D0968977

WORKSHOP ROTATION

A New Model for Sunday School

Melissa Armstrong-Hansche and Neil MacQueen

Geneva Press
Louisville, Kentucky

Book design by Sharon Adams
Cover design by Kevin Darst

First edition
Published by Geneva Press
Louisville, Kentucky

This book is printed on acid-free paper that meets the American National Standards Institute Z39.48 standard. ♾

PRINTED IN THE UNITED STATES OF AMERICA

00 01 02 03 04 05 06 07 08 09 — 10 9 8 7 6 5 4 3 2

Library of Congress Cataloging-in-Publication Data

Armstrong-Hansche, Melissa.
Workshop rotation : a new model for Sunday School / by Melissa Armstrong-Hansche and Neil MacQueen.
p. cm.
Includes bibliographical references.
ISBN 0-664-50110-9 (alk. paper)
1. Christian education—Teaching methods. 2. Sunday schools.
I. MacQueen, Neil.
II. Title.

BV1534 .A76 1999
268′.6—dc21 99-046804

CONTENTS

– Introduction –

Who Cares?

Who should care about this book?

Those who . . .

. . . wonder if there's a better way to do Sunday school.

. . . are dissatisfied with their current curriculum.

. . . are frustrated about finding (or being) teachers.

. . . are tired of bored students.

. . . have bland, unimaginative classrooms.

. . . think biblical literacy is important.

. . . are looking for ways to boost attendance and appeal to visitors.

. . . enjoy being creative.

. . . believe in teaching through various learning styles.

. . . are willing to risk change.

This list of needs, frustrations, wonders, and hopes was our own list. We've since discovered that it's just about everybody else's list too. In 1990, we began exploring a new approach to Sunday school at the Presbyterian Church in Barrington, Illinois. We called it the *Workshop Rotation Model.* Our kids and congregation called it "a great Sunday school." Every day we talk with teachers, pastors, parents, and Christian educators who are looking for something better for their Sunday school. This book is for them, and for you.

People often ask what prompted us to reinvent our elementary-age Sunday school. The answer is simple. Our program was in crisis: Low attendance. Difficulty in recruiting teachers. A basement facility that looked like a dungeon. An expensive denominational curriculum few teachers liked (and some never took out of the cellophane wrapper). We had joined the church staff within six months of each other, Melissa as the part-time children's director, Neil as the associate minister for education and fellowship. After watching the program run (or not run) for several months, both of us knew something had to change. Both of us were willing to risk failure in order to achieve success, and we found that our congregation felt the same way. Perhaps most important: both of us had children in the program.

Before coming to work at the Barrington church, Melissa had been a high school teacher and volunteer in charge of Sunday school in her home congregation. Melissa was the kid who grew up loving Sunday school. By contrast, Neil was the kid who didn't like Sunday school and rarely went. With different gifts and by different paths we found ourselves in the same suburban Chicago church in desperate need of a solution. In the summer of 1990 we sat down in front of a flip chart to figure out what to do about Sunday school.

Whatever we came up with, we agreed that it had to be workable for both volunteers and staff. At that time, Melissa worked at the church only ten hours a week. In addition to his responsibilities in children's ministry, Neil was involved in both youth and adult ministry. We value creativity, and we wanted to have a creative program. We knew, however, that the Achilles' heel of any church program is the amount of time it takes to plan it and recruit people for it. Creative models have come and gone precisely because they were unsustainable in a volunteer environment or heavily dependent on one or two creative people. We knew we wanted to do something creative, but we had to find a way to do so without burning out everyone, including us!

One option on our flip chart was to shut Sunday school down and do something else, rather than continue boring our kids into membership oblivion. We had heard of other churches doing just that—doing something different on another day of the week. We knew we were going to create some other opportunities, but we weren't ready to throw in the Sunday morning towel. We felt Sunday morning was an opportunity and a time slot too important to pass up. We also wanted to give Sunday morning our best effort before doing something so drastic. We believed if we built our dream program, the children would come.

And come they did! In our first year of the *Workshop Rotation Model,* we not only increased attendance, we created a second Sunday school hour during our second service to handle the demand. More important, our kids were learning Bible stories in a fun and memorable way, and they wanted to come back.

How does the *Workshop Rotation Model* work? In chapter 2 we'll describe the model in detail, but for those who can't wait, here is a brief description:

1. Your elementary-age classrooms are redesigned into creative, media-inspired, kid-pleasing workshops that teach Bible stories. These workshops can include: art, drama, audiovisuals, computers, Bible games, puppets, and music.
2. Classes or groups rotate to new workshops each week for four or five weeks, the "rotation" period. Workshop teachers do not rotate. They stay put in the workshop, repeating the lesson to a new group of children each week (with some age-appropriate modifications).
3. During that five-week period only *one* Bible story is taught. The entire rotation—every workshop, every week—is focused on learning that one Bible story.

That's the *Workshop Rotation Model* in a nutshell.

The first time we drew the model on the flip chart, it looked so simple we thought something had to be wrong with it. It addressed every problem we had listed. It looked too easy. And yet it is this simplicity that turned out to be one of the model's greatest strengths. We looked at our list of our wishes and problems. We looked at our solution and said, "Let's do it."

Of course, we did have to get permission from our committees and leadership. Surprisingly, that was easier than we expected. It reminded us of the story of the emperor with no clothes—after we spoke up, we soon found many of our members felt the same way we did about Sunday school. They had seen the same problems we had seen. They too were ready for change.

We started *Workshop Rotation* almost immediately, using summer classes to try out our new model and get our rooms together. When September came, we hit the ground running and haven't looked back since. We did tinker with our model for a year or two before telling other folks about it. Slowly but surely, other churches began adopting the *Workshop Rotation Model* for their Sunday schools. Most experienced the same or even greater results. It is now estimated that more than twelve hundred churches are using the model in a variety of settings. Some of those churches have successfully extended the model into their teen and preschool classes.

"Rotation churches," as they call themselves, are sharing their enthusiasm and materials across the country in every state. "The WoRM," as the *Workshop Rotation Model* is affectionately abbreviated, is increasingly well known in some church educator circles and is used in churches across the country, including many in the Chicago and Dayton, Ohio, areas, in northeast Indiana, and in parts of Wisconsin. Clusters of rotation churches can be also be found around the Denver area, central Florida, Philadelphia, Pittsburgh, Baltimore, Portland, Minneapolis, Oshkosh, Kansas City, Central California, Cincinnati, and St. Louis, just to name a few.

There's now a *Workshop Rotation Model* website (www.Rotation.org) with an online newsletter and an annual national conference (in addition to many regional events). While originally networked through Presbyterian channels, rotation has now spread to many other denominations. This is due in part to its adaptability and the realization that most Sunday schools, regardless of denomination, are experiencing stagnation or decline.

A dark hallway and an old exit door are transformed into the gates of heaven at the Presbyterian Church of Barrington, Illinois.

On the one hand, the *Workshop Rotation Model* represents a new approach, but on the other hand, many of the model's organizational and creative ideas have been floating around for years. For instance, some vacation Bible school curricula have used elements of the rotation idea in one form or another. Essentially, the model is a fresh and practical approach to organizing what we already know how to do: teach the Bible creatively. The *Workshop Rotation Model* is a combination of good ideas brought together at the right time.

The *Workshop Rotation Model* may be the solution you need for Sunday school. But we also think it represents something even more important than just a particular model. Models will come and go as needs and ideas change. The *Workshop Rotation* movement is about the willingness to risk change for the sake of doing something better. It's about creating a program that takes into account the limitations of our volunteers and allows their strengths to shine. It's about stopping the conveyor belt that's sending kids and their families right out the back door into membership oblivion.

Is the *Workshop Rotation Model* the right model for your Sunday school? Maybe so. This book will help you think through that question. The one answer we're sure most churches cannot afford is to continue doing more of the same. The evangelism of our kids is too important to their spiritual journey and the future viability of our congregations.

May God bless your ministry with his children.

— 1 —

What's Wrong with Traditional Sunday School?

Plenty is wrong with traditional Sunday school. Where are all those kids who were in Sunday school twenty and thirty years ago? Where are they now on Sunday mornings, and where are their children? Is it possible that the very programs we put them through are part of the reason so many have decided to stay away? Could their childhood experience of being bored in Sunday school have influenced their decision to walk away when they grew old enough to choose, and to stay away with their kids now? When they think of going to church with their kids, do memories of mildewed church basements, hard folding chairs, and lifeless lessons affect their enthusiasm and decision making? Of course they do. Even those who enjoyed Sunday school (or survived it) often have a difficult time getting their own children to go to Sunday school these days.

Today's parents are in some significant ways different from the generation of parents before them. Today's generation no longer accepts that old excuse for Sunday school, that it's like medicine: "bad tasting but good for you." This generation of parents is far less willing to support a program that leaves a bad taste in a child's mouth. They are the ones who grew up saying, "I'll raise my kids differently, you'll see!" Now in charge, they have transformed the public school experience from the rooms full of desks in a row to the dynamic multimedia classroom we see today. They expect teaching methods to be reasonably interesting, if not fun. And when they're not, they sympathize with their kids as did no other generation before them.

The church is experiencing a decline in volunteerism and institutional loyalty, in part because of the changing notion of commitment and the increasing number of things people want to commit themselves to. Our people have more options. It's not that people don't have the time to be great teachers. There are still twenty-four hours in a day. It's simply that they have chosen to do something else. They're spending more time at the soccer field, the club, at work, traveling, or just looking for time to spend at home. The pressure is on to find "family time," and in some households, time for just plain sleep. Options for kids are greater, too. Remember when the only thing on Sunday morning television was a news show and *Davey and Goliath*? With so many other opportunities, many in our churches are opting out of supporting church programs they find less-than-fulfilling.

Generations of learners enjoying the computer lab at Edwardsville United Methodist Church, Edwardsville, Indiana.

The "logistics" of church attendance have changed, too. The rise in single-parent households and the reality of children alternating weekends between divorced parents are new challenges to Sunday school attendance and teacher recruitment. The demise of the corner church has further distanced our members from us, both psychologically speaking and in terms of time spent in the car. Restful weekends have gone the way of the hula hoop. Sunday morning now competes for attention during the typical family's action-packed weekend.

These changing notions of commitment and volunteerism are true not only for parents, but for seniors as well. We all have more options commanding our attention, and we're less inclined to say yes to options that make us uncomfortable or that we find frustrating. However, rather than viewing this as a negative, we can see it as a positive. It has forced many churches and their Sunday schools out of a deep slumber.

Times have changed. Attitudes, needs, and educational styles are changing. The Sunday school needs to change as well or it will continue to forfeit ground in a battle it must not lose. Whether you agree or not with our assessment of the traditional model, the numbers and the struggles across the denominations are telling us that we need something more than the Sunday school model of the 1950s. For many churches right now, it is more than just a matter of vitality; it is a matter of viability. And the more Sunday school stagnates, the more it becomes an issue of viability for us all.

We need successful Sunday schools. When Sunday school fails, it fails more than just children. It fails the family, the youth groups, and the future of the congregation itself. When Sunday school fails, confirmation classes become crash-courses in Christianity, youth can't find the New Testament in the Bible, and teenagers become scarce in worship. When Sunday school fails, potential teachers go into hiding, and frustrated committees begin looking for the next "Holy Grail" of a curriculum to save the program.

When Sunday school languishes, ministers and church leaders who fund budgets and salaries don't take children's ministry seriously. Young families are less likely to join or stay active in the church. Parents do not get the help they need to raise their children in today's world. We fail the next generation of the church by providing fewer churchgoers and churchgoers who are less enthusiastic and more biblically illiterate.

When Sunday school attendance drops, denominational statistics begin to slide and, with them, the prospect of future mission dollars. Years after the Sunday schools fail, pastors head off to contemporary worship seminars to learn how to win back into the sanctuary many of the same people who were chased out when they were young.

But when Sunday school thrives, children are happy to be there and they learn more about the Word of God. The thriving environment tells them God is alive and welcoming. Attendance increases. Church-shopping visitors are interested in coming back and joining. Budgets and salaries get more support. Staff, committees, and teachers are happier and more creative. The purpose of this book is to share a model for revitalizing Sunday school. It attempts to address all these issues in a practical way. The *Workshop Rotation Model* is not, however, a panacea. It cannot overcome poor planning, uninspired leadership, or an unwillingness to change.

Sunday school isn't the only area of children's ministry in need of our attention. There are other important areas a congregation needs to emphasize to effectively evangelize its children:

Family Ministry. Children learn values and what is important primarily by watching and listening to their parents and siblings. If mom, dad, grandma, or older brothers and sisters don't care about their faith, the young children in the family probably won't either. Churches need to equip parents to be the primary Christian educators of their children. We need to provide Christian home-building resources. We need fellowship and mission opportunities in which families can participate together. The connection between healthy Sunday schools and healthy new-member classes must be recognized.

Children's Fellowship. This should be a vibrant,

joyful, playful, music-filled time to grow up in the presence of loving adults and establish relationships with peers whose families share similar values.

A Caring Minister. Children see ministers as the representatives of God (and sometimes early on even *as* God). Children need pastors who know their names and spend time with them beyond worship. Sadly, many pastors leave children's work entirely to others in the congregation. They fail to recognize that children's ministry is an opportunity to minister to the whole family.

Children in Worship. If children are not in worship, what is the purpose of all our Christian education? If they are not in worship, where will they learn to appreciate worship and be shaped by our traditions? If they are not with their parents in worship, how can their parents model worship skills and attitudes for them?

Youth Ministry. As our children become teenagers, they naturally begin to question their beliefs and consider pulling away. Yet many churches invest more in their youth ministry than children's ministry. By then, it is often too late to start. The best youth ministry we can create is a strong children's ministry to build on!

This list could go on. We hope it will jump-start the discussion in your congregation. Some successful resources, models, and solutions already exist. Many more are needed.

— 2 —

Problems, a Wish List, and a Solution— the *Workshop Rotation Model*

One hot June day, in an act of confession, we sat down in front of a flip chart and made a list of all the problems we were having with our Sunday school. That process in and of itself is worth doing if you haven't done it before. When we presented the *Workshop Rotation Model* to our church leaders, we took them through the same confessional process. What an eye-opening experience it was for us all.

Here were our main problems . . .

Teachers. Where did all our teachers go? Many of them had become working mothers. Early on in our search for a new model for Sunday school, we knew we could no longer depend on finding teachers who could teach for the entire year, or even for part of a year. Team teaching was only a partial solution. We knew we would still end up with Saturday night or early Sunday morning planning on their part. You certainly don't get creative lessons and enthusiastic students that way! We needed more from our teachers, not less. But they needed less, not more. We wanted the teachers to be even more creative and exciting. Where were we going to find them and how could we train each teacher to be the Bible scholar, audiovisual wiz, drama coach, art teacher, and game leader that traditional programs demanded? A teacher who has all these skills and the time to offer them is a rare find. One traditional excuse has been to blame the volunteers ("If only they would . . . " "Why won't they . . . "), and a typical response has been the attempt to train them within an inch of their lives. We knew that whatever we did, the teaching commitment had to be realistic. It had to bring out the best in them and make them want to teach again. Our solution had to involve more people, not just the faithful remnant.

The Curriculum. All of us, it seems, have been on a quest for the Holy Grail, searching for that one new-and-improved curriculum that can solve all our problems. Like other churches, ours had been trying different publishers' guaranteed remedies. These quests customarily begin with kick-off Sunday ballyhoo and end a few years down the road in a quiet whimper and renewed search. Our latest new-and-improved curriculum had failed us (or we had failed it), and it was expensive, not only in terms of dollars, but in lost time and opportunity as well. We decided that our solution wasn't to buy something else. We had a whole shelf full of "something else." Instead, we determined that the answer wasn't a new curriculum.

Our Classrooms. Our classrooms were sadder than sad. Furniture-choked rooms with beige concrete walls and faded construction-paper letters on crooked bulletin boards spelling out "_ESUS LOVES YO_." None of us would decorate our children's bedrooms like those classrooms. None of us would allow inadequate lighting and "basement mildew decor" in our schools. Why had we allowed it to happen in our church? Our kids didn't want to go down there. Even *we* didn't want to go down there. No matter what we taught, we knew it would be the kiss of death to put it all back into our uninspired classrooms. We wanted an atmosphere that expressed the love of God, not something out of Dante's "Inferno."

The Schedule. Our attendance, special event schedules, and teachers' availability varied throughout the year. We were paying for thirteen Sunday lessons a quarter, but we rarely had even ten free Sundays to teach them. We needed something that was flexible, adaptable, inexpensive, and able to ignite some enthusiasm while being faithful to the Word of God.

Bible Literacy. We wanted our kids to remember their lessons. We were tired of confirmation kids not knowing who, what, where, or why about the Bible. We questioned why we were moving too fast through the Bible, as if all our kids were there every week. We wondered if it were reasonable to be spending so much time in any other part of the Bible when our kids couldn't remember the basics about Jesus' life. We also recognized the need to go back over previously taught material. We needed to find out what didn't sink in the first time. We also knew that our students had a better chance of remembering their lessons if we refreshed their recall.

Apathy. We wondered out loud if anybody other than a handful of us takes Christian education seriously anymore. We wondered if the apathy affected not only our recruitment and attendance but also our budget, staff salaries, and leadership abilities. Worse, we could see the apathy reflected in the faces of our kids and parents. Few parents wanted to step into their kids' classrooms, and the kids couldn't wait to leave.

Attendance. Last but not least, we had lousy attendance. On any given Sunday, more than half of our kids were missing. And yet we bought the curriculum and our teachers dutifully prepared their lessons every week, as if everyone were there all the time. We knew there were many other factors that affect attendance (such as good preaching). New to the church staff, we were told, "Our families are just very busy."

Instead of making or accepting excuses about all of these problems, we believed we could do better. But how? We made a wish list:

1. We dreamed of a real art room in which to get messy, to concentrate our art supplies, and of a teacher who enjoyed teaching children through art (not just someone skilled in crafts). We joked about banning construction paper to see if we could live without it.
2. We dreamed of a drama and puppet area full of costumes and props and with plenty of room to put on Bible skits, and we envisioned an audiovisuals room where the kids could relax and view or act out God's word in something other than folding chairs or an old bathrobe.
3. In our dream program, each classroom and every hallway would be a visual treat, a place kids would love to be. We dreamed of a place and a program that would turn kids on to the things of God and the church, not turn them off. We wanted even the walls to teach, welcome, and comfort.
4. We wanted a model that didn't ask our teachers for an unrealistic commitment of time, training, or skills. We wanted a Sunday school that could tap into busy but creative talent in our congregation rather than depending on the ones who had the time or felt obligated to help.
5. We wanted to reduce our reliance on and expectations of expensive curriculum. Purchasing teacher manuals, flyers, and workbooks (which didn't always get used or enjoyed) was eating up our budget. We literally had a room full of creative resources collecting dust. Our teachers knew where these materials were, but they were hard pressed to use the denominational curriculum, let alone wade through all our other resources. The answer wasn't a thorough dusting, but a fresh idea about using some of those resources.
6. We wanted a model that spent more time on the more central Bible stories and not four weeks on "The Man

with the Withered Hand" or a winter in the minor prophets.

7. We wanted a curriculum schedule that took into account the fact that most children don't attend every Sunday.
8. We wanted a Sunday school modeled on the way children love to learn: through movement, smells and tastes, visual stimulation, feelings, games, and drama. We wanted an educational approach that was welcoming and fun, while at the same time being educationally sound.
9. We wanted our church leaders, parents, teachers, and other members to recognize how important Sunday school is to the health of the congregation. We needed from them no fear of failure and every encouragement.
10. The last thing on our wish list was the fortitude and prayers to make the necessary changes! We knew from the outset that what we were asking for was not out there and that we would probably have to create it. We were determined to go forward—wherever forward might lead us. Staying the same was not an option.

Do any of these problems sound like your problems? Is your wish list similar to ours? If so, read on for a solution that just might make your day.

A SOLUTION: THE *WORKSHOP ROTATION MODEL*

Wrestling with our dreams and frustrations, we set out to create a program that addressed as many of the items as possible on both lists. We looked at other models, adapted a few ideas, and came up with a couple of our own. What emerged was what we called the *Workshop Rotation Model*. The phrase "workshop rotation model" is usually used only by those who are describing the model to others. Some churches call their rotation Sunday schools by locally inspired names, such as "New Bible Adventures," "Spirit

Trek," and "Bible Discovery Zone." In our congregation, we called it "Sunday school." Within a couple of years, "Sunday school" was synonymous with "awesome!"

The Changes We Made for Grades One through Six

The *first* thing we changed was the assignment of grade levels to the same room each week. We redesigned our former classrooms into a collection of creative learning–based workshops through which classes or groups of kids rotated, one workshop per week. In our church, we have the art workshop, the drama and puppet workshop, the audiovisual workshop, the Bible skills and games workshop, the Bible computer lab, and the music workshop. Each of these workshops, which will be described in more detail in chapter 4, has its own unique decor, furniture, and layout to facilitate the mode of learning that takes place. Following a posted schedule, the children rotate to a new workshop each week. Each workshop teaches the same Bible story that the others are teaching for four or five weeks at a time.

The *second* thing we changed was the assignment of teachers to specific age groups. Instead of teaching a new lesson each week to the same class for all or part of the year, rotation teachers are assigned to one workshop for each four- or five-week rotation. They prepare one lesson using a lesson plan that our design team has given them (more about the design team in chapter 7). Since they use the same or a similar lesson each week as the different grade groups rotate through, the teacher needs to prepare the lesson only once and then repeat it each week. During the rotation, the teachers make age-appropriate adjustments, using suggestions from the lesson plan. They also make adjustments based on their experience from the previous week. By the second or third week in the rotation, rotation teachers know their lesson plan by heart and have improved it based on real classroom experience. This frees them from constantly looking at the manual and allows more focus on and eye contact with the students. Lessons sound less "canned" since they're not read off the page. The teachers also like the shorter length of commitment. Now they say, "Five weeks? I can handle that!" and come back for more.

Many churches recruit caring adults to move with each group of students through the workshops as the class "shepherds." Shepherds see to the pastoral needs of the kids, helping the workshop teacher as needed. In our church, we originally had a designated "shepherd" for each class. But due to some of the unique circumstances and strengths of our congregation and Sunday school, we soon dropped the shepherding idea. Most of our rotation teachers taught several different rotation periods during the year and became well known to our students. Depending on your church's circumstances and needs, you might include shepherds in your design.

The *third* change the *Workshop Rotation Model* makes is repeating the same story through different learning media for four to five weeks in order to increase Bible literacy. Repetition is the cornerstone of remembering. Students learn the same story each week through a different workshop medium. This multimodal approach targets the many learning styles of students. Because the story is presented each week in a different workshop with a different teacher and medium, the students don't get bored. In fact, we found our students felt good about remembering the story from week to week. This also allowed our teachers to explore the story in more depth as the weeks went on. This slower pace was especially beneficial to our infrequent attenders. When they came, they got a great lesson. Because we were taking our time on the major stories of the Bible, their exposure to those stories increased.

The *fourth* thing that the *Workshop Rotation Model* changed was our schedule. Instead of having to combine or eliminate lessons in order to keep up with a traditional quarterly curriculum, the rotation lesson schedule is set by the church. The length of a rotation can be adjusted to adapt to such factors as the church's calendar, how many workshops you want to use with the teaching of each story, and how many weeks you want to spend teaching it. Most churches have found that four or five weeks is a good rotation length. This allows them to cover the story in depth, to achieve Bible literacy, and to minimize preparation time for the teachers. A church with six grade groups in the rotation can teach a three-week rotation about the birth of Jesus, if that is all the time they have between Thanksgiving and special Advent Sunday programming. They will still need six workshops for the six groups, but for that rotation each grade group will miss three of the workshops. Conversely, a church with only two or three grade groups can study the prodigal son for as many workshops as they can muster. This flexibility in adapting to the church's schedule, the number of workshops, and the number of grade groups makes the *Workshop Rotation Model* usable for programs of any size or on any schedule. You can view sample workshop schedules in chapter 9.

The *fifth* change was eliminating the need for frenetic eight-step lesson plans. The rotation model uses simple three- or four-step lesson plans. The reason? It takes time to do a Bible study and then reenact it as a drama, or watch a video, or create a wire sculpture, or do Bible research on a computer, or set up a puppet play on the Bible story. Traditional eight-step lesson plans often turn the teacher into something of a ringmaster or juggler. With a simplified lesson plan, the teacher's focus is off of the manual and on the particular learning activity that the teacher is skilled at teaching. Teacher stress level is reduced, and there is less tendency to lecture. Plus, there is more time for teacher-student interaction because the teacher isn't always trying to figure out what to do next or running around looking for supplies.

The *sixth* change the rotation model brings is the elimination of a reliance on expensive prepackaged curriculum. Lesson plans come from a design team of creative volunteers who glean from other resources and come up with their own ideas. Finding one creative art project every five weeks is a whole lot more doable than coming up with a creative new project every week. The *Workshop Rotation Model* also recognizes that individual workshop teachers will modify some of what we give them and improve on the original lesson plan week after week. The money saved by not buying expensive packaged curriculum gets plowed back into the program for other projects, props, costumes, computer software, bright paint, and creative decor. The *Workshop Rotation Model* brought us excitement, Bible literacy, improved attendance, happy students, happy teachers, improved interactive learning, new volunteers, renewed support for the program, and ownership of the education process. One of the best results was with our visitors and new members. Our Sunday school became the number-one reason people said they continued to visit and eventually join our congregation. "Our kids didn't want to go anywhere else," they told us.

The *Workshop Rotation Model's* facility makeover isn't merely window dressing. It's about providing a stimulating place to learn. It's about evangelizing today's families. In the next several chapters, you will read more about each aspect of the *Workshop Rotation Model.* But before sharing more details about "how" it works, in the next chapter we'd like to suggest "why" it works.

A historical note: The *Workshop Rotation Model* has many things in common with some vacation Bible school programs, learning centers, and other creative curricula developed over the years. We agree with Solomon that there truly is nothing new under the sun. We've run into educators who "did something like rotation back in the nineteen-whatevers." What makes the *Workshop Rotation Model* unique is the combination of certain ingredients and a slower pace, allowing creativity to be sustained over the long haul without burnout. We've asked educators why they think this model is taking off now and why the church didn't latch on to it decades ago. Many longtime educators have pointed to the timing. The past two decades have shown us what happens when Sunday school isn't done well and when it burns out creative people. The *Workshop Rotation Model* comes at a time when many Sunday schools and congregations are exhausted and in decline. They need to do more with less. They are looking for effective, attractive, and yet more practical solutions to their problems.

WHAT ABOUT TEENS AND PRESCHOOLERS?

Most rotation educators believe preschoolers should not be included in the rotation model because they need the same room and the same teachers each week. It is true that preschool curriculum, materials, and furniture needs are quite different from those of older groups. However, a close look at a typical preschool curriculum reveals that this age group often, in effect, does use a kind of rotation: the children move among learning centers. Moreover, preschoolers are attracted to the rotation scheme, and it is not uncommon to see preschoolers sneaking into an empty workshop to make use of it from time to time.

As for teens, in Barrington, we had good attendance and participation in our youth Sunday school classes. So we didn't try to fix what wasn't broken. Other churches have had some success bringing junior highs into the rotation; a few have even brought their senior highs into it. Teen classes need a few modifications to fit the model. They need more mature lesson materials and teachers who know how to handle the age group. Many rotation churches with rotating teen classes send a special teacher along with the class. Others have their teens use only some of the workshops, such as the computer lab or the audiovisual workshop, and then have them return to their regular classroom and discussion mode.

Teens often make better teachers than students. They make great "Bible lab buddies" and drama team leaders. Those churches that have included teens in their rotation often did so after a year or so of limiting their rotations to the elementary grades. Even when teen classes joined the rotation, they often did so only for two or three weeks, skipping certain workshops to do other things teen classes like to do.

Based on experience, we recommend leaving teens out of the *Workshop Rotation Model* until you are ready for them. Over a couple of years, you will be "graduating" rotation students into the teen classes. In time, they will come to view the rotation as a normal way to do Sunday school, making it easier for you to bring their age group into the rotation schedule as warranted.

What about adults? One of the more exciting developments we've heard about has been the use of the model with adult classes and intergenerational groups. In starting up the model, however, we suggest you keep it simple at first.

WEEKNIGHT USE OF THE *WORKSHOP ROTATION MODEL*

Many churches use the *Workshop Rotation Model* to organize their Wednesday evening fellowship, in addition to or exclusive of the Sunday school. With more regular weeknight attendance, they typically have shorter rotation periods of perhaps only three weeks per story. Workshops are often bracketed by dinner, game time, and worship times. In churches where the space cannot be completely converted into workshops, the weeknight workshops often store their materials in media boxes for easy transport. Quick transformations of classrooms into fun workshop environments can be done with a collection of curtains, theater flats, tents, and so on. You can read more about shared-space solutions in chapter 9.

– 3 –

Why the *Workshop Rotation Model* Makes Sense

It makes sense because it works! It helped us meet our educational and evangelistic objectives. Now for those who need more reasons why it works, here they are. . . .

Reason One: It is practical for the teachers and fun for the kids.

Imagine yourself as a volunteer teacher in the *Workshop Rotation Model.* You are approached to teach three rotation sets a year, a fifteen-week commitment. The first two rotations work into your schedule nicely and you get a scheduled break before your last five-week "tour of duty" during November. During the first two rotations, you are in the art workshop because you love teaching with art. Nobody knows this about you (yet), but you had a minor in drama at State U., so for the third rotation you decide to tackle the good Samaritan story in the drama workshop. No running around on Saturday night. No fumbling through your teaching manual on the way to church. The kids can't wait to see what they're going to do in your workshop. And if it doesn't turn out well your first week, you get a "do-over."

Now put yourself in the shoes of a fourth-grade boy (carefully). You come on Sunday, eagerly anticipating which workshop you'll be assigned to and not knowing exactly what you'll be doing. You're greeted at the door to the Theater

Workshop (audiovisual) with a bag of popcorn. The next week you learn you will be going to the Bible computer lab! Later that month, Mom asks you to name all the Ten Commandments, and after you've reeled off nine of the ten (Mom could only remember seven), Dad asks you which workshop helped you learn them best, "The one where you made the Commandments clay tablet or the Ten Commandments Computer Quiz?" Then on your way out of church you hear a rumor going around that next month your class is going to go to prison with the apostle Paul.

Costumes and props make the resurrection story come alive at the Presbyterian Church of Barrington, Illinois.

Reason Two: It emphasizes the learning environment.

We believe that the first lessons children learn from Sunday school are whether or not they are welcome and whether or not there is anything here to be excited about. All of us learn from and react to our surroundings. This is particularly true of children. Children "read" the environment we create for them, and these impressions help shape and shade all the lessons that follow. Researchers tell us that among children (and many adults) these subjective readings of the learning atmosphere have a strong emotional component. Feelings are created and rekindled by sight and smell. Feelings about the teacher, the room, and the lesson activity become linked to their feelings about God, the church, and the Bible.

Think about it for a moment from a child's perspective. What might spiders and mildew, dark hallways and ugly walls be saying to the child about God? What does forty-five minutes in a folding chair do to a child's feelings of welcome, and how much of that translates to how a child feels about the Bible being used in that atmosphere? Does the soul feel rocked in the "bosom of Abraham" by steel furniture and cold tile floors? Some might feel this analysis is overstated. But others, including your authors, believe we have not taken such contributing factors seriously enough.

We took these "first lessons" to heart and committed ourselves to transforming our Sunday school surroundings, regardless of what model or curriculum we came up with. We wanted our kids to feel God's love and warmth even from the paint on the walls. Our former beige and block basement became a feast for the eyes. Outside the workshops, colorful Bible story murals abound. The children are greeted by smiling Bible characters and a large display area signaling the rotation theme. Old furniture has been stored elsewhere or thrown out. Dark corners have been lighted. Fresh pictures and posters have been hung. "Church clutter" and poorly used bulletin boards were removed. Signs were posted for visitors. Old or broken fixtures (lights, hardware, faucets, doorknobs, vents, etc.) were fixed or replaced. Banners were brought out of storage. And most significantly for asthma and allergy sufferers, that mildew smell has been eradicated!

In the central hallway of our Sunday school area, we removed the old chairs stored there and painted a mural of Jesus and other Bible heroes. We spent a lot of time thinking about the facial expression and body language of Jesus, because we knew children would be looking and learning. Artistically, we made sure the resulting mural would be of lasting and impressive quality. Our sense of "first lessons" was confirmed by a father in our congregation. He brings his preschool son by our Jesus mural every Sunday. "He has to see Jesus," said the dad. "He loves to touch the mural." This transformation has happened with enthusiastic support.

An inviting Jesus and heroes of the Bible welcome children in the central Sunday school hallway at the Presbyterian Church of Barrington, Illinois.

Even our trustees came to understand the needs of children and saw that this wasn't going to be the "same old." When the program makeover was presented to them in terms of attracting members and keeping current members active and educated, they enthusiastically joined with us. They appreciated the fact that we were saving money on a curriculum by using our own resources or less expensive ones. They saw how excited the children were to be learning in the workshops. Several of them said they wished it had been like this when they were kids or when their own children were younger.

The rule of thumb for the transformation of classrooms into workshops is simple: form follows function. Let the medium of the workshop and the activities you will conduct there guide your redesign of the space. Our audiovisual workshop has theater seats, not folding chairs. (Many churches have found free or inexpensive seats from theaters that were remodeling.) There's a popcorn machine in the corner and Bible movie posters on the walls. The drama workshop has cushions and couches to sit on, with plenty of floor space so we can create any scene we can imagine.

The more traditional learning environment of the Bible skills and games workshop has plenty of "gameware" and a large, white sheet draped underneath the fluorescent lights like a tent. One large wall was painted to look like the interior of Solomon's Temple. Some churches have stipple-painted every concrete block in their room to look like Temple walls. Others have created a "scripture tent" or "synagogue" right in the middle of their room.

No two workshop rooms are alike, and they are not unchangeable. From time to time, we convert rooms into all sorts of exciting places. For a rotation on Paul, we turned a small room into a prison cell using paper drop cloths on the walls and ceilings, straw on the floor, and cardboard "bars" on the door. A Roman guard stood at the door during the entire class time, completing the effect and offering some interesting dialogue!

Because we believe atmosphere to be so critical to the learning process, we spend quite a bit of time making our rooms exciting places for the kids. Because we don't have to spend our budget on an expensive curriculum, we have money to spend on the little extras that can mean a lot. When you look at your rooms, think big, think different, think like a kid. In chapter 4, you'll read about more room ideas.

Reason Three: The *Workshop Rotation Model* uses multiple learning styles to teach the Bible.

Some students learn better by doing or saying, moving or sitting still, viewing or hearing, touching or tasting, discussing or pondering. In fact, we all learn through all these different styles but through some styles more than others. The human brain is a multisensory marvel, soaking up input from its external world, arranging and linking it in countless ways at multiple levels. The more multisensory the learning, the more broadly and deeply it is stored and recalled. Because the brain is wired this way, conscientious teaching must be wired this way as well in order to make the most of our students' capacity to learn and grow.

Educational research tells us that children tend to be more visual learners and kinesthetic (movement) learners in their childhood, with the capacity to listen and learn (auditory learning) not fully developing until puberty. Certainly Jesus knew his listeners had different learning styles. Look at the way he dealt with the rich young ruler versus the

Drama workshop, DeSoto Presbyterian Church, Dallas, Texas.

woman at the well, or blind Bartimaeus. Of course, Sunday schools have always known about learning styles. Even many traditional curricula have been creative in their approaches. The *Workshop Rotation Model* simply slows the pace down, making the lesson planning and execution less an impossible task for the teacher.

In recent years, public schools have put theory into practice, redesigning their classrooms and curriculum to better complement children's learning styles. They have also done it in recognition of how teachers teach. Many elementary teachers team together, rotating their classes to the one teacher who best teaches social studies, math, or science. Even junior and senior high schools employ this concept, with teachers teaching in their area of strength instead of being required to be jacks-of-all-trades. The issue isn't whether different learning or teaching styles should be used; we've always used various styles. The issue raised by the *Workshop Rotation Model* is how best to organize our Sunday schools to take advantage of different learning and teaching styles. The discussion of reason four, concerning teachers, elaborates on some of these points.

Reason Four: The *Workshop Rotation Model* recognizes our teachers for who they are, and who they are not.

It's a game of chance when we hand manuals to volunteer teachers with little or no training and then give them a class of kids for the semester or year. Even when we pick good teachers with good teaching and relational skills, traditional-model teachers still have problems.

> "Bill won't have his class do the art project because he's all thumbs."
>
> "Jill can't sing a note, so she doesn't use the music part of the lesson."
>
> "Bev would rather lecture and skip the games because she thinks they're too childish."
>
> "I don't know why Ted came unprepared; usually he's on top of things."
>
> "She didn't have time to get the props together so we're going to watch a video instead."

Sound familiar?

The *Workshop Rotation Model* recognizes our teachers for who they are, not what we wish them to be. They don't always do a good job. They are not always as prepared as they should be, and left on their own with a lesson plan, they will pick and choose the activities that make them feel most comfortable. The *Workshop Rotation Model* identifies the gifts of our teachers (and their weaknesses) and puts them in a workshop where their talents can best serve the kids. The weekly repetition of the lesson lets them improve and feel better about their teaching experience.

The ability to have a "do-over" is perhaps the single most powerful and compassionate aspect of the model. This power and compassion extend right into the lesson plan itself. Traditional lesson plans try to do too much. They try to jam too many styles of learning into each lesson. This creates lesson plans with six or more elements to be used in a class period of forty-five to sixty minutes. This is a recipe for teacher frustration and student overload. One could also make the case that this overload did not work in terms of Bible literacy or attendance.

In the *Workshop Rotation Model,* class content and lesson plans are pared back to just a few elements. Each workshop teaches a complete lesson through its own particular style or medium, using teachers skilled in those styles. After six years of teaching with workshops, it has been our experience that children and teachers don't get bored by the slower pace and the repetition of the story. On the contrary, they relax, interact, have fun, get more involved, and get more time to think and do and talk. As the weeks progress, knowledge and understanding improve.

Last but not least, the *Workshop Rotation Model* doesn't ask for unreasonable commitments from our volunteer teachers. Whether you agree with their reasons or not, most of our church members will not make (or do not have) the time to teach traditional Sunday school. Most churches find themselves drawing from an increasingly smaller pool of prospective teachers. This is poor stewardship of member teaching talents. The rotation model offers our members an easy-to-digest commitment. It gives them an opportunity to teach children in their preferred style. Rotation churches report new teachers coming out of the woodwork, a sign of their support for the program.

Reason Five: The model is adaptable to churches of different sizes and different facilities, and to different theological points of view.

In our first year of operation, we didn't give much thought to whether or not our model could be used by other churches. We were simply doing something that worked in our situation. Slowly but surely, however, other churches began giving it a try. One of the first of these was a church half the size of ours with only a part-time director of Christian education (our church had nine hundred members when we started the *Workshop Rotation Model*).

Gradually, the rotation model has found its way into churches of all sizes and circumstances. The smallest church we know of doing the rotation model has forty-one members. The largest has more than six thousand members. Interestingly, it was a six-hundred-member church that helped the six-thousand-member church by sharing their first-year materials and insights. Because workshops replace classrooms, most churches do not have a "where do we do it" problem. In fact, many churches have extra space due to membership decline and a larger facility than the Sunday school needs. Smaller churches, however, often have only two or three classrooms to convert to workshops. Spurred on by the creative problem solving that the workshop approach engenders, these churches have adapted the model quite successfully to their situations. One room might pull double duty as a drama workshop one week and an audiovisual workshop the next—more about this in chapter 9.

The *Workshop Rotation Model* embodies a theological point of view. It seeks to make the Word of God attractive and memorable to young people. It makes Sunday school more like heaven than purgatory. It believes in our members' giftedness and recognizes their limitations. The rotation model says that it is the responsibility of each congregation to determine the content, scope, and sequence of the curriculum. You will see a suggested six-year plan in this book, but it is not an eleventh commandment. This model encourages ownership and responsibility for a process and content that we believe is within the talents and gifts of each congregation, no matter the size.

Having said that, it is surprising how much consensus there is across the country and denominations about which Bible stories and concepts should be taught. We encourage each church to go through a discernment exercise—to gather church leaders and let them decide (and thus, own) their Sunday school's content. We have our own particular thoughts on what we think should be taught through the rotation model. You can find our scope and sequence in chapter 6.

Practical, flexible, adaptable, kid-pleasing, teacher-friendly, inviting, informed by different learning styles, aimed at producing Bible literacy, and educationally sound—that is the *Workshop Rotation Model,* and it works!

– 4 –

The Workshops

In this chapter we describe the five main workshops in our church and provide descriptions of many other creative workshops as well. How many workshops you create will depend on the number of weeks you want a rotation to last (five weeks means five workshops are needed) and how many groups you want to have rotating each week. It may also depend on how much space you have or your Sunday school attendance. Small and large church variations are discussed in chapter 9.

THE ART WORKSHOP

This was the workshop that got it all started for us. We wanted a real art room, the kind we had in school when we were kids. The wonderful materials, the colorful projects hanging from the ceiling and walls. The smells. The paint on the tables (and on the floor). The sense of excitement we had just walking in the room thinking about the possibilities.

In our art workshop we feature display space for completed projects, track lighting to augment (and overcome) fluorescent lights, a wall unit full of terrific art supplies in full view of the students. The walls are brightly painted, and so are some spots on the floor and tables. Clunky and confining church school chairs have been replaced with art stools. This allows us to seat all the different size students who use the workshop. Art stools are easier to move and slide under the table as needed. Stools allow students to work closely together and let teachers get closer to their students without having to stumble over a chair.

Art workshop Bible stories are first read and then discussed around the table. Then the teacher introduces the art project to the students, explaining what it is about the project that connects with the story. We emphasize "art" over "craft." No coloring pages, crafts-in-a-bag, or popsicle-stick Jesus puppets here! A craft project is one in which the student imitates what the teacher does. Craft projects usually consist of a lot of construction paper and glue and could just as well be called "time killers." Art projects are more complex. They require thinking and expressing, not just cutting along the dotted line and lots of pasting. Art projects allow a student to manipulate the materials to express the story.

Art projects not only capture the student's imagination, they also capture parents' attention and tend not to end up on the floor of the car or in the wastebasket at home. They have "shelf life." One terrific example of a *Workshop Rotation Model* art project is making prodigal son wire sculptures. After studying the story, the students are given a wood base, and they staple flexible wire to it. Then they bend the wire to represent the characters in the parable. The characters are posed to express their role and feelings in the story. Throughout the sculpting, the teacher moves among the students, discussing their individual projects and what they are trying to express. After everyone is done, it's sharing time.

The wire sculpture art project illustrates something else about the art workshop. Different age groups will use art materials at their own level. Given wire, younger students will make simple sculptures, older ones more complex. The same is true for paint, clay, mosaics, and other materials. Good art materials allow individual students to work at their own level. Craft projects, such as construction paper and cut-along-the-dotted-line handouts, last about five minutes and often amount to busywork.

The key to the art workshop is to pick quality projects and recruit artistically inclined teachers. Art workshop teachers discuss the Bible story and its meaning with the students even as they are involved in the creation process. We call this "the patter." Every art lesson plan provides "talking points" to the teacher, things to talk about before, during, and after the project. In Sunday schools of years past, the teacher would typically stop the discussion and move into a craft activity, too busy cutting felt and scrambling to find more markers to continue teaching the story. In the art workshop, the art activity is central to the lesson and frees the teacher to discuss meaning rather than the material.

Because teachers get to repeat the project week after week, they don't have to scramble for materials or worry about getting done in time. They know how long it takes after the first week. Because the project stays the same each week, materials can be stocked in quantity and left out for next week. Because the project changes only once every five weeks or so, teachers and lesson planners can afford the time to find quality projects. Many rotation churches tap into their local art communities and the pool of artisans in their congregation for new project ideas, materials, and help. Art projects create discussion in the class and at home. We no longer have problems with children wanting to race out at the end of class. More likely than not, mom and dad wander in to see what their child is working so hard on.

There are many wonderful and inexpensive Christian education resources for art projects. They also often come with complete Bible studies. Your church probably already has a shelf or closet full of resources and materials. Art workshops go by many names in rotation churches. "Creation Station" and "Thou Art" are two popular titles.

THE DRAMA WORKSHOP

Children are born actors. At just about any age, they love to dress up and put on a skit. Sunday schools have harnessed this opportunity, energy, and imagination for decades. We wanted a real drama room, not a classroom with a box of old bathrobes in the corner. We needed space to move around in, not furniture to stumble over. We wanted a real stage area, not a corner in a room or a cardboard-box puppet theater.

Our drama workshop has its own stage lighting (inexpensive "clamp" lamps), curtains (fabric sewn together and suspended by shower curtain hooks on a wire), backdrops (theater flats and wall murals), and a closet full of costumes. Walk into our prop closet and you will find Jesus' tomb, Roman soldier gear, moss-covered rocks (burlap and paper sacks), baskets, pottery, shepherd crooks, pillars, trees, a copy of the Ten Commandments, and many other wonderful items that kids enjoy selecting. Even the selection of props is an opportunity for discussion about the story.

In the drama workshop we often use a style of teaching called "interactive drama." The class first reads and discusses the Bible story, and then creates a script or outline. They talk about each character and scene, choose props and costumes, and then walk through the drama. The teacher acts as guide, director, prompter, and questioner. In this interactive style, the teacher will say things to the characters such as, "Why don't you want to go to Egypt, Moses?"or "Why do you want Moses to go to Egypt, God?" In large classes, the story can be split

Drama workshop, Zion United Church of Christ, Sheboygan, Wisconsin.

among or repeated by several small groups. Every student gets involved. Even the shiest students will agree to be a sheep.

Sometimes the class divides up for discussion and then comes back together with contemporary skits based on the lesson. Occasionally a ready-made script is used, something from a creative curriculum or drama service. Most of the time, however, students must create their own script as part of the learning process.

Videotaping the dramas for immediate or future playback is a great way to focus their attention on the work, and they love to see themselves on screen. It also provides a focus for further discussion, prompted by questions like, "Why did you say it like that, Saul?"

THE PUPPET WORKSHOP

Anyone who doubts the educational power of puppetry has never seen *Sesame Street.* Even adults love puppets. Puppets are a powerful teaching medium since they let students express themselves in an indirect way. Puppet plays, like dramatic presentations, help students reconstruct and remember Bible stories as well as express meaning and emotion. Yet puppets have hung on the fringes of Sunday school, largely because the average teacher is unskilled in the medium or doesn't have the tools to do puppetry well.

Enter the puppet workshop. There is a teacher who understands and enjoys the medium. Our volunteer-made puppet stage is large enough to accommodate several puppets, a curtain, and two stage lights. Some rotation churches go all out, with large, professional-looking stages constructed with black cloth hung over plastic PVC pipe structures. These larger stages allow students to walk and stand with their puppets rather than crowd in behind the smaller stage that's familiar to most churches. A large seating area on the floor in front of the stage is often strewn with big cushions. Puppets of all sizes and shapes are readily available. After studying the Bible story and creating a script, students select

Bible character or contemporary puppets, hand puppets or larger arm puppets to rehearse with.

Inexpensive puppet scripts are also helpful. Younger children love to recreate Bible stories on our puppet stage. Older children enjoy putting on puppet shows for the little ones. Having an adult or youth present puppet plays is another possibility for the puppet workshop.

We often combined the puppet and drama workshops, depending on the year, the story, and teacher availability. For some rotations we had our younger children use puppets and the older children do a drama. You can purchase puppets, and there are many helpful resources on teaching with puppets. Check your local Christian bookstore, resource center, the Internet, or children's ministry conference.

Puppet Workshop Variations

1. *Make your own puppets.* Many puppet workshops get their kids involved in making their own puppets. This can be time consuming but rewarding.
2. *Marionettes.* Some cutting-edge rotation programs have found that their older students enjoy the challenge of dramatizing Bible stories with marionettes. The complexity of movement focuses their attention. Some older students also tend to view simple puppets as "little kids' stuff."

THE AUDIOVISUAL WORKSHOP

Imagine a room with theater seats and a popcorn machine, and you have one of our most popular workshops. We bought our old seats at a fire sale (literally, some of the seats had smoke damage). Free used theater seats are one of those great secrets you now know about. Every time a movie house or auditorium remodels, the seats are up for grabs. We put ours on a raised wooden platform. And what would a theater be without popcorn? The smell alone is enough to bring the kids running!

The audiovisual workshop is straightforward: children

learn by watching quality presentations and then discussing them. Almost all of the Bible's great stories have been put on film and are easily available. The kids love the Cecil B. De Mille action. You just can't beat Victor Mature as Samson, or Charlton Heston as Moses. Many fine "Jesus films" are available from which to glean clips. Some great animated Bible stories are also on the market, with more coming out all the time. (Note: While showing brief clips for educational purposes is usually allowable, showing some videos to a class in their entirety may be a violation of copyright. Check first.)

The audiovisual workshop can also be a place where children make and show their own audiovisuals related to the rotation story they are studying. Cartoon cells, filmstrips, slides, and videos—they're all in play now. In the past, such projects usually took too much scrambling for resources. The rotation model gives you a workshop stocked with creative materials that are always at hand and being used.

The audiovisual workshop at the Presbyterian Church of Barrington, Illinois.

Let's hope we've all gotten beyond the "video babysitting" label and come to understand the power of moving images to shape the mind. Viewing and creating audiovisuals can be powerful teaching and memorization tools. The *Workshop Rotation Model* makes the most of this learning style by recruiting a teacher who knows how to properly use the medium. As in other workshops, the audiovisual workshop begins with Bible study, then turns to a visual medium to work the story deeper into our students' minds. Throughout the use of a video or creative activity the teacher is working with the story, asking questions. Audiovisual teachers know that the pause button on the VCR remote is their best friend. Because a video or creative audiovisual project can take most of the class time, this workshop is one of the easiest for first-time teachers.

The audiovisual workshop concentrates all the Sunday school's audiovisual equipment in one place. Unlike some churches where you have to sign up for equipment, in rotation churches you won't find teachers vying for the VCR on Sunday morning. The audiovisual workshop can also be a place to make audiovisuals, such as filmstrips, videotapes, cartoon cells, and cardboard TVs with Bible scenes drawn on butcher paper scrolls. There are mountains of resources on making audiovisual materials. This workshop gives your church the place to make it regularly happen.

A few rotation churches have split off the making of audiovisual materials into their art workshop and turned their audiovisual workshop into a viewing experience. Many rotation churches call their audiovisual workshop the "Bible Time Theater." One calls it "Reel to Real" (or is it "Real to Reel"?) They decorate the walls with movie posters (such as for *The Ten Commandments, Prince of Egypt, Jesus Christ Superstar,* etc.). Paint schemes and decor include painted film frames on walls and ceilings with glow-in-the-dark

"More popcorn, please!" The audiovisual workshop at the Palma Ceia Presbyterian Church, Tampa, Florida.

stars. Some theater workshops have comfy couches or cushions on the floor.

THE TV NEWSROOM WORKSHOP

This workshop forms an interesting hybrid between audiovisual and drama workshops. We never had the space to do this workshop, but we always liked the idea. Broadcasting from the Newsroom on WFPC (W. First Presbyterian Church), for example, this workshop takes its cue from those time-honored "man on the street" interview skits found in many youth program resources. But it goes the old standard one better. The workshop is outfitted like a TV studio, complete with an anchor desk, cue cards, and video cameras on tripods. Corners of the room provide backdrops for many famous Bible scenes where on-the-spot reporters interview the Bible characters and events as they happen.

It's amazing what a little imagination, cardboard, paint, and cloth can do! Like the other workshops, the TV newsroom begins with basic Bible study, followed by discussion and creation of a TV news program. Roles are given out and the program rehearsed. Then the news reports are videotaped, not only to have a record of the fun, but to provide direction and cohesiveness to the process and content. "Now back to you in the newsroom, Chet . . . "

THE BIBLE SKILLS AND GAMES WORKSHOP

This workshop teaches the rotation story or theme with traditional paper, pencils, books, and maps, but also through the use of fun games and projects. While teaching each rotation's Bible story, the skills and games workshop emphasizes where and how to find the story, Bible geography, Bible culture, and how the story fits into the larger biblical story.

A retired man in our church built a game-show "buzzerbox," complete with flashing lights, for our workshop. He also made us a "Wheel of Fortune" spinner. We draped a sheet across the fluorescent lights for a tent-like effect. We dug out all our old maps and charts from "gone and forgotten storage," mounted them on foam-core board, and hung them all over the walls. This makes them accessible to the teacher and to the inquisitive eye of the student. On one wall is a large hand-painted and illustrated map of the Middle East for the kids to use to locate their Bible stories. Maps are great "graphic user interfaces" for many stories of the Bible (Abraham, Exodus). They help students organize and understand the material in a different mode.

A mural of Solomon's Temple adds visual depth and vibrancy to the Temple Workshop (Bible Games) at the Presbyterian Church of Barrington, Illinois.

This workshop uses the only room in our Sunday school with conventional tables and chairs. However, at times even these were removed when we turned the floor into a giant game board or transformed the room into Esther's palace.

As with most of our workshops, we gave our Bible skills and games workshop a special name, the "Temple School." In the room was an ugly, rough foundation wall. We painted a mural of the inside of Solomon's Temple on it, hung curtains on either side of the mural and pretended that we were sitting in a "balcony" inside Solomon's Temple for class. Like all the murals in our Sunday school, the Temple mural told a story. We left the doors open to the Holy of Holies so the kids could see the ark of the covenant. All our kids know that in Solomon's day, those doors should have been closed, but they know that Jesus opened the way to God.

Many rotation churches have even created an ark of the covenant for their temple workshop. They paint the individual concrete blocks in their room to resemble the wall at the Temple Mount, leaving the top part of the wall sky blue. Palm trees sprout in the distance and caravans can be seen heading out of Jerusalem.

Colorful Bible murals are common in rotation churches in hallways and in the workshops. Some churches are blessed with local artists who paint their murals. Others copy scenes onto transparencies, which are then projected on a wall, traced, and painted. Many Bible skills and games workshops are held in "Scripture tents." These room-size tents have floors covered in Persian rugs and cushions. Such tents are especially helpful in workshops that must be taken down for day care or to hide something stored in the room. Another variation is called "The Synagogue." At the beginning of the lesson, the students file into an ancient synagogue constructed inside the room. Prayer shawls and head coverings in place, the students sit on wooden benches, listen to the daily reading and participate in prayers and discussion. Afterward, they may retire to the outer part of the room for a Bible game linked to the reading.

A storyteller begins a lesson at Palma Ceia Presbyterian Church, Tampa, Florida.

Some churches use a version of the Bible skills and games workshop called the storytelling workshop. Here students listen to a practiced storyteller in a bible-times setting, such as a Bedouin encampment.

"The Tent Commandments," "Temple School," "Bedouin

Encampment"—the names and themes for the Bible skills and games workshop are as endless as the imagination. The *Workshop Rotation Model* makes creative decor the rule rather than the exception. You can devise Bible games on just about any story or theme. You probably have a shelf full of activity books in your church already.

Tabernacle Workshop (a.k.a. Bible Skills and Games Workshop) at DeSoto Presbyterian Church, Dallas, Texas.

THE MUSIC WORKSHOP

Music is perhaps the strongest, most emotionally influential medium we have to work with. Hook the Bible story to a song, and it is rarely forgotten. And yet many Sunday schools struggle to find teachers able to tap into this powerful gift. It is not uncommon for teachers simply to skip the music sections of traditional lesson plans. Knowing this, many publishers seem to be excluding music altogether from their materials.

The *Workshop Rotation Model* offers a way to get music back into the teaching of Bible stories. When kids rotate into this workshop, they find a teacher who really knows how to get the kids singing and having fun (no choir practice allowed!). "Father Abraham" might get them spinning and wiggling. An old favorite makes them feel welcome and familiar. We love to sing Christian campfire favorites, because they are fun and their words stick with you throughout your life.

The content of this workshop *is* the singing, wrapped

with some brief study and some "talking points" (like, "What are the seraphim doing falling down on their faces before God in the hymn 'Holy, Holy, Holy'?"). In a recent rotation called "What Is God Like?" we sang "You're a Great Big God," followed by an introduction, singing, and discussion about the hymn "Holy, Holy, Holy." "Make a Joyful Noise to the Lord" was the theme of another workshop that taught Psalm 150 and included instrument making.

We use our choir room for this workshop. Other churches convert a room into a music workshop just for the kids. Because some Bible stories don't lend themselves to music (try finding a song about Ruth), many rotation churches schedule the music workshop only as needed. Because music is one of the most powerful teaching mediums, you will want to put it to use somewhere in your rotation. If you can't support a music workshop, look for time before or after class or during the week to use this important learning gift.

THE BIBLE COMPUTER LAB

Welcome to our kids' favorite workshop! Computers are wonderful new learning tools. Someday, we expect them to be downright traditional. The funny thing is that our kids think they are. Computers are not new to this generation, only to the older generations in the church. When combined with the right software and the right teacher, the attractive power of computers makes for an exciting lesson.

We really went out on a limb when we first started teaching with computers in 1990. We were searching for new mediums to use in our rotations. A member volunteered to buy us two 386 PCs, knowing how much his own kids loved to use them at home. Now it was time for our education! Almost immediately we were overwhelmed both by the kids' ecstatic reaction and the parents' positive support. As one of our teachers put it then, "Now all we have to do is learn how to *teach* with them!"

Computers are still a relatively new idea in Sunday

school. Many teachers have never taught with software and sometimes the decision makers are computer illiterate. This is becoming less so. Several realities are making the idea of computers as tools in our Sunday school easier to imagine:

Most churches have more computer-literate parishioners than biblically literate parishioners! And this certainly goes for the children as well.

Computer prices continue to fall, and many church members have computers, including laptops, to contribute.

The quantity and quality of Christian education software has improved.

More churches have begun teaching with computers; thus we have a better track record and source of advice.

Many church offices have computers capable of running Christian education software.

More and more, computers are seen as an acceptable and essential part of our educational and cultural landscape. You don't need one computer for every student in the lab. Your Bible computer lab can be as small as that one computer sitting idle in the church office on Sunday morning. Or it can be a whole room dedicated to computer-assisted learning.

We began with two PCs, which eventually became five, loaded with about seventeen different Christian software programs. These programs include computer Bibles, creative writing and drawing programs to recreate the stories on screen, quiz-making programs to test and reinforce our students' comprehension, multimedia Bible storybooks, kid-friendly Bible research tools, memory-verse games, and computer games that teach Bible content.

Bible computer lab classes begin with face-to-face discussion and Bible study. The software is used in much the same way as art projects, videos, music, and drama, that is, as a component in a lesson plan, not as a replacement for one. No kids "zoning out" in front of computer screens here! The teachers are right beside the students, working through the

"WWW.Faithjourneys.org," the computer lab at DeSoto Presbyterian Church, Dallas, Texas.

software with them.

Other lesson activities may be brought in to round out the lesson plan. For example, a study of the journeys of Abraham and Sarah might take students through a Bible atlas program, then on to create a wall map tracing the events of the journeys. Following the creation of the wall map, students might finish up the Bible computer lab with a computer quiz on the content of the day's lesson.

Especially in their first year of the method, many rotation churches find that they cannot afford the software to cover every rotation story (or the software doesn't exist for that story yet). Generally, we recommend that the Bible computer lab be allowed to evolve and not always be tightly tied to the rotation. Some excellent software programs need more than one week to work with. A growing number of rotation churches give their older students more than one week per month in the lab. This is accomplished by a little creative scheduling.

Bibleland.com, Bible Computer Country, Digital Disciples and the Keyboard Kingdom, From BC to PC—Bible computer labs go by many names. Wherever you find them, you'll find a group of kids who don't want to leave. [Note: For more specific information on teaching with computers, visit Neil MacQueen's website at www.sundaysoftware.com.]

OTHER WORKSHOPS

The *Workshop Rotation Model* has unleashed pent-up creativity in many congregations. New workshops are being created to go with certain stories or certain teachers, or just for a specific year. Some become permanent workshops. There are mission workshops, cooking workshops (e.g., Mary and Martha's Bed and Breakfast), even a "Matters of Faith" Science Workshop where kids create experiments that demonstrate the rotation story's meaning. Much of this growth and expansion is the result of teachers and staff gleaning from their own creative resources. Ideas that once seemed like an awful lot of work now are within reach. Because of its creative flexibility, the *Workshop Rotation Model* calls forth all sorts of creative lesson plans and themes. Many were possible in the past but too difficult to squeeze into the curriculum and teacher's schedules. Now you can design an entire workshop around that great idea or creative resource.

One of our favorites was a workshop on the apostle Paul. Taking a break from the "one story per rotation" rule of thumb, we turned our different workshops into towns or places that Paul visited. One small room was draped floor to ceiling in brown paper. The floor was strewn with straw with a canvas drop cloth underneath. We took the door off the hinges and substituted a cardboard jail cell door in its place. Outside the Ephesus jail cell we stationed a very convincing Roman guard who "captured" the young Christians who had assembled outside for the workshop, chained their legs to each other (with black decorative lamp chain) and tossed them all in the pokey, where they found Paul and Timothy. It was an experience they long remembered. The effort was possible because we knew it was not just for one lesson, but for five. And each week the drama and dialogue between the soldier and his Christian captives was improved upon.

VARIATIONS

Depending on your topic, schedule, available space, and personal preferences, the *Workshop Rotation Model* can be customized to suit many needs. For example, some churches can't support a forty-five–minute music workshop, so they include music in their Bible skills and games or drama workshops. Some rotation churches have combined their computer lab with their Bible skill and games workshop. Most churches, however, find that these two workshops have plenty to accomplish on their own.

One of the beauties of the model is that you can configure the number of workshops and grade levels in rotation any way you want. The one fairly constant number in the model is the number of weeks appropriate to teach a story. Most churches, like ours, have found that four or five weeks works out best. Sometimes, due to special events in the life of the church, rotations can be as short as three weeks. Any less and you lose the cumulative effect of teaching the same story through various mediums.

Some years and for some rotations you might choose to combine your drama and puppet workshops. It really depends on your available resources and what you want to accomplish.

Some churches gather their children together for a "pre-workshop" assembly. The assembly can take many forms. It might have the look and feel of children's worship or be used to introduce or further illuminate the rotation story, perhaps enacted by a "performance troupe." Songs can be sung, journal entries written, mission projects worked on, and announcements made. After assembly, children go to their different workshops. A few rotation church schedules permit the entire group to reconvene for a closing assembly. One limiting factor is the amount of time you have on Sunday. Another is the average amount of time it takes to complete an art project, put together a drama, watch a video, or complete a software program. Generally, your workshop should be at least forty to fifty minutes in length.

Congregations have many class sizes and schedules to accommodate. The *Workshop Rotation Model* has proven to be very adaptable to almost every Sunday morning schedule, Wednesday evening schedule, class size, budget, and space limitation.

In our church, we needed to create two Sunday school hours to disperse our attendance. It either was that or build bigger rooms! Our second-hour class sizes were smaller, so we broadly graded them and ran three workshops at a time during the second hour over a five-week period in order to stay even with the first-hour rotation story schedule. This meant that on any given week, two of our five workshops were empty the second hour. (This is the schedule with which many small rotation churches operate all the time.) We asked the first-hour teacher to stay over and teach the second hour. In the spring, attendance dropped, so we sometimes broadly graded both hours.

Because the *Workshop Rotation Model* draws so heavily on local ideas and gifts, program details can change from year to year. Such variations often depend on how much time and space you have, in addition to your great ideas!

– 5 –

Reactions from Teachers, Students, Staff, and Congregation

Before discussing the curriculum, we'd like to share with you more details about the exciting results that we and others have experienced teaching with the *Workshop Rotation Model.*

TEACHERS

How our teachers love to teach in the workshops! That's because . . .

We ask them for shorter commitments, four to five weeks at a time.

We place them in a workshop most suitable to their skills. No more frustrating "jack of all trades and master of none" teaching.

They have to plan the lesson only once because they repeat it each week for a new class with small adjustments for age appropriateness (something that teachers who are parents do naturally).

They are no longer frustrated and stressed by late-night planning.

They know that if for some reason they don't get all the way through a lesson, the basic story will be repeated the next week in the rotation.

As the rotation progresses, they can build on what

the children have already learned in the other workshops.

They get better and better each week as they repeat and modify their lesson.

Other churches that have used the model have reported similar success. Their teachers have experienced similar feelings of relief and renewed energy. Because their students are happier, they are easier to teach, and that makes the teachers happier. The model has addressed many of the teachers' long-standing complaints and frustrations, particularly those about time demands and difficult lesson planning.

Churches also report tapping into a new group of volunteers excited by the possibilities of something different for them and their children.

THE STAFF

For us as staff persons, putting creativity at the core of the program was a dream come true. In the past, it was frustrating to come up with creative ideas, only to have those ideas poorly used or not used at all by an unprepared, hurried teacher who didn't have the time or the tools to be creative. Now, each teacher's lesson is centered on one stimulating and creative activity.

More benefits for the staff are rooms that look great all the time and not just when the teacher has time to get around to decorating them. The art supplies are always in the art workshop. The VCR is always ready in the audiovisual workshop.

This model rests on a belief in simple lesson plans that count on the workshop medium to do a large share of the teaching (the song, the movie, the drama), and this frees us from dependence on annual purchases of curriculum. We now know that the teachers are teaching what we want them to, as opposed to the old days when the teacher might ditch some if not all of the lesson and teach something else. And with several weeks of workshops on the same story, we get a chance to correct things that looked great on paper but did not turn out so well in practice.

Perhaps most important, because our kids are happy, the teachers are happy, and that makes the staff happy. Work? Yes. But that is nothing new to Christian educators. What is new for rotation educators is the way we find ourselves energized by happy kids, Bible literacy, improved attendance, and happier teachers. Our creativity is nurtured and our spirits fed.

THE KIDS

Kids love the *Workshop Rotation Model.* What's not to love? They get something new to look forward to each week. They don't need to be dragged to church by nagging parents. They get learning activities that are fun and a prepared teacher. They get exciting rooms. And they feel good about learning and remembering God's Word. We now have very few discipline problems compared with the old days of sedentary curriculum. Nobody wants to miss out on the neat stuff. Workshops capture and direct their energies; too often traditional Sunday school gave them a reason to entertain themselves by acting out to combat boredom. Workshop activities allow them to wiggle and squirm, get up and move around.

Imagine this: we now actually have kids waking their parents up on Sunday mornings so they can get to church! Our kids have stopped watching the clock in the classroom. They don't want to rush out at the end of class. The workshop Sunday school also has had a profound effect on how our children act in worship. They feel more at home and attentive in a place they enjoy. Because they have something neat to look forward to, they better tolerate the times when the service takes on a more adult atmosphere.

THE PARENTS

Our parents used to approach Sunday school with a "grin and bear it" attitude, but no longer. The majority of their children now love to attend church. Instead of "My kids don't want to come," we hear, "My kid woke us up this morning for church." One father stopped to ask how we had taught his girls to remember the Ten Commandments (through a computer game). He happily admitted how embarrassed he was on the ride home from church that day when they quizzed *him* on the Ten Commandments!

Most telling is the change we see in how the parents act on Sunday morning. They used to stand at the door and say, "We have to go home now." Now, parents walk in to see what their son or daughter has been doing (and probably wants to stay and finish!). Many families have told us that our children's program was the main reason they chose our church over others. This support has translated into increased attendance, volunteers, and financial support.

THE CONGREGATION

Congregations will tolerate mediocre Sunday school. They've grown used to low expectations. But they love terrific Sunday schools! Many of our older members especially love the sight of happy kids in church. The kids' joyful presence has created goodwill, support, and patience when we wanted to try something new.

VISITORS AND NEW MEMBERS

Visitors are looking for churches that offer something biblical, innovative, and exciting for their children. Many of those visiting our church have told us that their kids have said to them, "We'd better join this church." One young boy convinced his mom and dad to let him stay from nine to noon and let the neighbors bring him home, all because he loved church school and wanted to repeat the workshops and go to worship again (no kidding, and in a Presbyterian church!).

CHURCH OFFICERS

When we went to the session (the governing officers of our church) asking to implement this model, we went loaded for bear. Charts, figures, budgets, handouts. After we stopped talking, the clerk of session spoke up: "Well I think it's great; my kids grew up in the church and they hated Sunday school." One after another our lay leaders said, "Go for it." They too knew that something had to change and that we had little to lose but so much to gain.

INCREASED ATTENDANCE AND OTHER POSITIVE RESULTS

Another important result reported by rotation churches is an increase in attendance of anywhere from 10 to 60 percent. One church tripled its attendance in three months: they only had three kids to start with and soon had nine! Quantity counts. We are in the evangelism ministry. But there are so many other factors that can affect attendance. Some congregations and neighborhoods are going through troubled times. Poor implementation of the model can certainly affect results. The *Workshop Rotation Model* is not a panacea. It's a philosophy of doing better. It's about understanding your problems and coming up with practical and attractive solutions.

All over the country great results are being reported. For some it is the boost in attendance. Others point to the care of teachers, emphasis on Bible literacy, or the unleashing of creativity. We attribute most of the positive reaction to a deeply held, if not often expressed, belief in the need for good Sunday schools. One St. Louis church, known for having a good traditional Sunday school, switched because, they said, they believed in "moving forward, not standing still." For them, the *Workshop Rotation Model* was an evolutionary step.

A surprising number of educators and pastors report almost no resistance to implementing the *Workshop Rotation Model*. In many congregations, it is as if the people were simply ready and waiting for it.

– 6 –

The Curriculum—Our Six-Year Plan

"Sunday Schools tend to teach information rather than transformation."

This startling critique of Christian education was delivered during a lecture at our church by a Christian education consultant. We wrote down these challenging words and stuck them to our bulletin board. They hung there for years.

Transformation . . . how does that take place? To a large degree, all of us are the agents of God's transforming power. Certainly information is a part of that transformation process: the transformation from ignorance and agnosticism to the love of God and obedience to his will. One might even say that information precedes transformation in a two-stage process. Many lesson schemes teach this way: study the Bible; then discuss a commitment, a change.

But how does change really happen? How do our children learn of the love of God and the fellowship of the Holy Spirit? We believe that on Sunday morning this first happens through the way we make them feel welcome and happy to be in God's house. This is a *Workshop Rotation Model* cornerstone. If kids experience our atmosphere and curriculum as boring and uninteresting and our teachers as unprepared and frustrated volunteers "doing their duty," if they experience their learning environment in negative ways, all of this becomes an unintended lesson. The ultimate consequences of this unintended lesson can be devastating to their future contacts with the church and their faith in God. Thus, Sunday school teaching must first be stimulating and enjoyable. The transformation process on Sunday morning begins not in the head but in the heart, in the eyes, through the smells, sights, sound, and feelings people have when they encounter the people of God in the house of God.

If our kids don't want to be in Sunday school, they will find a way not to come back. Churches do not have the luxury of compulsory education. Many churches can no longer afford to play hard to get. We've driven an entire generation of kids through our Sunday schools and right off the membership cliff. And yet, some just assume that this is the way it's going to be—kids suffering for Christ in their folding chairs. And we've literally bought into the idea that published curriculum is necessary, even when we don't like it and are looking for our umpteenth new one. Nope, you can't teach a kid who doesn't want to be there, or who isn't there. We have to *reach* before we can teach. Traditional Sunday school knew this, and so it tried to interrupt the boredom with "Super Sundays" and occasional razzamatazz. Bore them, but at least bring doughnuts.

The *Workshop Rotation Model* seeks to "reach by the way we teach." Thus, this model goes beyond the dichotomy of "information" and "transformation," as if they were two separate things. Instead, rotation thinking creates a synthesis: we teach information in a transforming way.

Workshop Rotation Model lesson plans are transforming because they are presented in an inviting and stimulating environment where students experience a sense of anticipation. They are transforming because they are presented by teachers who have gifts for teaching in their workshops and who don't have to spend time in the class with their heads buried in a manual. Rotation lessons are transforming because they tap into the way the brain likes to learn, in a multimodal fashion. The *Workshop Rotation Model* is transforming because it pays attention to all the ways a learner learns. And last, rotation is transforming because it plants Bible stories, one at a time over a period of time, so that they can be carried by the learner far beyond the classroom to places where they can continue to unfold.

DEVELOPING A MULTI-YEAR PLAN FOR YOUR ROTATIONS

Most rotation churches develop a six-year rotation plan similar to the example in the section that follows. A six-year plan allows the church to determine what Bible stories an elementary student will learn before moving on to youth classes. Some churches develop three-year plans, teaching nearly the same stories twice during a child's elementary years for maximum retention. The length of your plan is up to you. One thing is for sure: no matter what you plan, you will most likely change it as new ideas and needs come into play.

To create our six-year teaching plan, we formed a task force to lay out all the Bible stories and Christian concepts we wanted to teach. This task force included teachers, pastors, parents, and members-at-large. We called it our "Grand Plan Committee." After brainstorming a long list of Bible stories and concepts and consulting other resources, we prioritized, shifted, and shaped a six-year scope and sequence.

It was a fun process. It created ownership and a sense of responsibility. It also let people know we weren't kidding around. It is a good idea to map out a rotation schedule several years into the future. The process of selecting which Bible stories to teach and in what sequence is challenging and enlightening. Bring leaders and members of your church into the discussion. If an important story or concept doesn't fit into the rotation schedule, find a place for it in some other program, such as weekday fellowship, confirmation, family events, special classes, or children's sermons. Six years may seem like a lot of time, but in reality you only have about forty-two rotations in a six-year period (seven rotations a year). This figure includes time out for holidays and special programs (five Sundays a year). These forty-two rotations do not include summer Sunday school. If your church has summer Sunday school, you will have about sixty rotation periods in six years, give or take a few.

Many rotation churches treat their summer rotations a little differently, due to irregular and low attendance. During the summer, you can plan abbreviated rotations or other special classroom experiences.

We made sure to place major stories during high-attendance periods. We also took into account the fact that some stories, characters, or concepts lend themselves to more than one rotation. The exodus, for example, was split into three rotations: one on Egypt, one on the Ten Commandments, and one on the desert wanderings.

Rotations of Jesus stories, for Advent, and for Holy Week were planned for every year. Our feeling was that if our kids did not know the story of Jesus, the rest of the Bible didn't much matter. We made sure to pick *stories,* not just one-liners. When a theological concept was chosen, we immediately asked what story would best teach that concept in a memorable way.

A SAMPLE SIX-YEAR WORKSHOP ROTATION PLAN

Year 1:

The Ten Commandments, the good Samaritan, the Christmas story, the prodigal son, Ruth, the parable of the talents

Summer: Stories about Kings

Year 2:

Abraham and Sarah, the parable of the sower, the wise Men, Esther (standing up for faith), the Lord's Prayer, the Lord's Supper, Psalm 8

Summer: Favorite Stories about Jesus

Year 3:

The call of Moses, Isaiah the prophet, Jesus as Messiah, Jesus in the wilderness, Good Friday, Paul (conversion)

Summer: Creation

Year 4:

Joseph, Psalm 121, Jesus the Prince of Peace, Jesus the healer, Resurrection, Paul as prisoner for Christ and letter writer

Summer: King David stories

Year 5:

The exodus, Elijah/Elisha, Jesus the Son, Jonah, Peter, church history/Presbyterianism

Summer: Miscellaneous Old Testament stories

Year 6:

What is the church? What is God like? the Beatitudes, Lent/temptation in the wilderness, Paul the preacher and tentmaker, Jacob and Esau

Summer: Life in Bible times

We used this plan at the Barrington Church, but it is important to note that this sample plan is a guide, not "gospel." Some traditional content may be missing from our Sunday school list because we present it in another program, such as our Wednesday Children's Fellowship. Some churches like to group and teach their stories in sequence, such as teaching Abraham, Jacob, and Joseph right in a row during one year. We chose to split them up. The choices are yours.

Notice that stories of the life and teachings of Jesus are central to our plan. The story of Jesus' passion is taught every year as a prelude to Easter, with an emphasis on one part of the story each year. We also identified Moses and David as the central Old Testament stories that children should know. The exodus story needs several rotations just to cover it all. We like teaching about Bible people: the stories of Ruth, Esther, Abraham, Paul, Peter. Children (and adults) relate better to stories and characters than to lessons boiled down to one or two verses.

Pertinent details behind each listing were kept in a notebook and a set of flip chart pages that we saved from the "Grand Plan" meeting. Some rotations, such as, "What Is God Like?" eventually became a rotation on the Trinity.

Later, we found that our kids still needed some help with the concept of Holy Spirit. So we did a rotation on the Holy Spirit and also talked about the Spirit in a series of children's sermons. It is surprising how quickly six years at a pace of eight stories a school year (not counting the summer) can fill up. After slotting in Advent and the Passion of Jesus every year, and teaching multiple rotations on large stories, such as the exodus, the number of open rotation slots is reduced even more.

Our plan pays some attention to the liturgical year and even more attention to attendance patterns. Some stories and concepts are more important than others for children to learn; thus, we teach them during higher-attendance time slots. There are times during the year when a three-week rotation fits better than a five-week one, such as just after Thanksgiving and before Christmas. Sometimes we broadly graded our groups. Sometimes we broke out of the *Workshop Rotation Model* for something different.

During the summer our Sunday school, like most, experiences more sporadic attendance. Workshops during the summer are broadly graded and are sometimes only two weeks long. During some summers, we take some workshops "off-line" to give them a breather or a facelift. The summers are also a time to use some of our favorite resources or stories that don't quite fit into any of the rotations. We might also teach some of our favorite Bible stories that are lower on our priority list (like Samson) and use the outdoors as a workshop.

TEACHING STORIES

The traditional model with its new-story-every-week approach is a clear case of "more is less" when the result is that the kids can't remember half of what they were taught. When you teach a Bible story in a memorable way, the story can grow up with the child, unfolding its meanings through all the child's developmental stages. The story lives in the child's memory and can be compared to the story the child is living. When children know the prodigal son story, then when they too become prodigals, the story tells them what to expect of God.

As you can see in our sample six-year plan, we did teach "concepts" or "themes" but almost always through a story. Most of the time we used the same story in each workshop on a given Sunday, though occasionally we added a story or a verse to certain workshops, depending on our lesson objectives and creative ideas. Some people criticize the *Workshop Rotation Model* for its emphasis on teaching through stories. We believe this is one of the model's strengths. Teaching stories is the best way to ensure that children carry their lessons with them when they walk out of the building.

– 7 –

Nuts and Bolts: The Design Team, Lesson Plans, Teacher Recruitment and Training

THE DESIGN TEAM

In our church, we created a design team of three to four persons whose job it is to follow the six-year plan, writing creative lesson plans for each workshop. The team meets quarterly for about three hours, working on two or three rotations at a time. After engaging in a Bible study, the team brainstorms lesson concepts and activities for each workshop. We often arrive with creative resources pulled from our shelves, frequently including complete lesson plans. Ideas are talked about and modified. Scripture verses and lesson objectives are written out for each workshop. Sometimes an idea or need is farmed out to someone beyond the team. The brainstorming sheets are then converted into lesson plans. Some lesson plans take shape in one or two minutes. Others are given to someone on the team for further work.

With practice and experience, we found that our design-team process produced exciting teaching approaches that none of us could have conceived of alone. The design process created ownership and empowered our volunteers. Over time, we have found that several essential types of skilled people are needed on the design team to produce a curriculum.

The Educator. You need someone who knows how to write lesson plans or who can learn to do so.

Fortunately, most churches are blessed with professional teachers among their members.

The Theologian and Bible Student. You need someone who knows the Bible well, someone who can offer brief scholarly commentary and background and can help identify the central theological concept in the Bible story.

The Brainstormer. You need someone who is a fountain of creative ideas. And your team must be able to brainstorm without the fear of hearing, "That doesn't work for me."

The Gleaner. You need someone who can wade through the many wonderful published resources for Sunday school and pull ideas for your design-team brainstorming sessions.

Of course, all of these skills may be present in several of your team members. We point them out to emphasize the set of skills needed for sound and exciting lesson design. Don't forget other creative people you can turn to for ideas and help. Who are the carpenters, artists, computer techies, interior decorators, and thespians in your congregation? Who can turn your cardboard into "Temple room" marble? Who can paint a mural of the Sea of Galilee for you?

OTHER WAYS TO PRODUCE LESSON PLANS

There are other ways of producing lesson plans. Several rotation churches we know of recruit teams of teachers for each workshop. Each team is given the overall theme and goals for a rotation and develops its own lesson plan for the rotation story. Several churches have staff or volunteers with special lesson-writing gifts. Others make regular use of the resource centers. Quite a few go back through their "old" curriculum with a pair of scissors and a file box. Some rotation churches have several different talented individuals who take turns writing the plans for specific rotations. Others have a team develop the basic outlines of the lessons and then hand them to workshop teacher teams that get together every couple of months to finish detailing the lesson plans. However you might choose to do it, it is important to keep the process open, recognize other people's gifts, and not become dependent on one or two people to create all the material.

One of the nice discoveries in the *Workshop Rotation* movement is the willingness of churches to share their rotation lesson ideas and plans. If you do not already know a rotation church, one visit to the *Workshop Rotation* website (www.rotation.org) will put you in touch with people and places offering free lesson materials. Some educators have the gift of creativity—that's what brought many of them to their role in the church in the first place. Other educators are better at finding creative people. Most churches have members who know how to write lesson plans, have great ideas, and have plenty of teaching experience. Our congregation was blessed with creative teachers and committed volunteers. Not only did the *Rotation Model* unleash these talents into our program, it gave these people the satisfaction of serving God with their gifts. We found we could glean from a lot of great resources.

As professional church educators, the authors have more than twenty years of experience between us, plus a seminary degree and a teaching certificate. But up until 1990, we never knew we had it in us to plan a curriculum and write it with the help of volunteers. Some churches purchase rotation curriculum. There are a few companies and churches that sell their plans. These offer the comfort of knowing you have something more polished to hand to your teachers. The *Workshop Rotation Model* is for those churches that have people with lesson-writing gifts and which want to give them the chance to exercise those gifts. Even those who purchase their lesson plans can enjoy modifying them to suit local needs.

RECRUITING TEACHERS

After lesson plans are created, teachers are recruited. Since it is important to match teaching strengths with the appropriate workshop, it is a good idea to have different recruiters for individual rotations or workshops. By spreading the recruiting job around, your recruiters will tap into their own groups within the church.

Rotation teachers are recruited per rotation, usually a five-week period. However, it is a good idea to ask your teachers to sign up for several rotations throughout the year. This will give your program consistency and improve their teaching abilities. We had many teachers who were regulars, often teaching several rotations in a row before taking a break. Many were happy to experiment by taking on workshops outside their usual preference. We encourage it. We look for individuals of mature faith and with an ability to relate to children. We encourage their input and changes to the lesson plan within the parameters of the overall workshop theme.

One of the things we have found is that good teachers who naturally relate to kids don't need to be spoon-fed every detail and every question or thought to interject into the classroom. We believe strongly in encouraging our teachers to be "serendipitous," that is, moving where the Spirit moves them in discussion and activity. Often, the best teaching moments are the ones that cannot be planned. Instead, they can only be reacted to with a "seize the moment" enthusiasm and skill. Creative teachers are opportunistic in the best sense of the word.

Because we have a number of repeat workshop teachers, the children experience about the same number of adults teaching them as in a typical team-teaching setup. Because the staff takes regular turns at teaching, the children get to know us as teachers, instead of just "pencil pushers" and offering collectors.

At first, we were reluctant to give up the traditional concept of the kids getting to know one teacher over an extended period of time. In practice, however, rarely were we able to find teachers who could volunteer this amount of time. Even in the rare cases where we did find this person, there were no guarantees that he or she would be a good teacher in any or all of the learning styles called for by the curriculum. In addition, even if the teacher could volunteer the time and was a good teacher, this didn't always make the teacher prepared, didn't always make the room inviting, and didn't help the other classes who were stuck with mediocre or poor teachers.

In the *Workshop Rotation Model*, you can retain your former teachers who still want to volunteer large amounts of time. We have found that their skills become focused in the workshop of their choice. When good teachers have the luxury of focusing their efforts, then *all* the children benefit from their expertise.

TRAINING

Once lesson plans are complete, we recruit teachers and meet individually with them to discuss their lesson plan and encourage input. Individual contact with them encourages their improvements while making sure that the lesson plan stays on track with the rest of the rotation.

Many rotation churches meet with their teachers as a group. Training rotation teachers can take many forms. One of the best ways to train new teachers for any workshop is to invite them to join an experienced teacher for a week or two. The rotation model offers a bit of "cover" for training teachers who need time to develop. In the traditional classroom model, inexperienced teachers can drive students away. In the rotation model, the teacher isn't the main focus, and we can match inexperienced teachers with a medium they find comfortable. The opportunity to repeat and tinker with their lessons also allows them to improve faster than in a traditional program.

During a rotation, staff or design team coordinators check in with each teacher to see how things are going and, if necessary, make additions, suggestions, and deletions in the lesson plan. Nothing is carved in stone. In addition to a lesson plan packet, many rotation churches create teaching guides or manuals for each workshop. These are kept in a notebook in each workshop for future reference. You can see several such manuals at the *Workshop Rotation Model* website (www.rotation.org).

FACILITY TEAM

Rotation churches frequently have a small group of creative folks who oversee transformation of classrooms into workshops. After the initial redesign, these volunteers sometimes evolve into a group of workshop coordinators responsible for keeping the rooms stocked with supplies and ideas. Facility team members can also be called upon to set up workshops for individual rotations as needed.

– 8 –

Rotation Lesson Sets

Writing lesson plans for a six-year plan is not difficult. Most of us, with a good library of resources at hand, can find eight or nine creative art lesson plans a year. Because we're teaching major Bible stories using familiar creative media, the odds of finding excellent ideas already in print are very high. It just takes time, planning, and creativity—things most Sunday school leaders are accustomed to providing. But creating lesson plans is an aspect of the model that scares some people. The trick is to find those people in your congregation for whom coming up with lesson material is second nature.

We brought to the *Workshop Rotation Model* a belief that lessons should be simple. We were teaching Bible stories to children, not rocket science to graduate students. We believed that if we taught the basic story and meaning in a memorable way, it would continue to teach them long after.

As rotation lesson writers we discovered that lesson objectives and activities could proceed at a more relaxed pace because we had more than one week for the story to sink in. We knew our teachers, given the luxury of planning one lesson and getting to repeat it, were going to improve on everything we gave them. We also found that, as the weeks unfold in a rotation, most of our students know the story better, a fact that didn't escape our teachers. Because of this teachers would evolve their lesson plans throughout the rotation period.

Once the design team has brainstormed and developed the lesson outline, it is time to create a lesson packet for each workshop and distribute it to the teachers. Each packet will contain notes on the entire rotation concept so that teachers can see what the design team was thinking. The packet should also contain the rotation title, dates, story background materials, scripture references, and "rotation overview." This overview, a list of what all the workshops will be doing, is essential to your teachers since they need to know what the lesson activities are in the other workshops.

EXODUS ROTATION OVERVIEW

Rotation Objective:

We've taught rotations on Moses' call, the Exodus through the Red Sea, and the Ten Commandments. This rotation will help students understand the whole scope and sequence of the Exodus.

OVERVIEW CHART

Workshops	Story Focus	Learning Activity	Teachers
Audiovisual	Story sequence	Watch several vignettes from *The Ten Commandments* videotape	
Art	Geography of Exodus	Make a relief map	
Computer	Geography of Exodus	Bible Atlas program plus quizzes	
Drama	Story sequence and how the people felt during the Exodus	Seven scene drama	
Temple	Story sequence	Jigsaw puzzle of story pieces	

The rotation overview also lays out the sequence of the workshops. One of the strengths of the model is that you can decide when an age group will be in a workshop. We usually place our younger grades in the audiovisual and drama workshops early in the sequence so that they can see and act out the whole story before getting to other workshops where the whole story may not be as apparent, such as in the art or computer workshops. Bible story background notes can be provided by the design team or pastor. These can also be found in a variety of handy resources, including a good study Bible or a Bible dictionary. Because our lesson objectives are simple, straightforward, and for kids, we have not found a need for the tremendous amounts of background information typically found in a store-bought curriculum.

During the meeting with rotation teachers (see "Training," chapter 7), materials needed for their workshop will be discussed. Depending on the workshop and the need, the materials may be provided by a rotation coordinator, staff person, or the teacher.

LESSON PLANS

Many resources explain how to write good lesson plans. Those new to this process may want to review an old curriculum. The steps of a lesson plan are known under various titles according to the conventions of the writer. In general, the parts of a rotation lesson plan include:

The lesson title

The rotation Bible story/scripture lesson

Some Bible background comments

A one- or two-sentence lesson objective

Lesson plan:

1. Opening activity (optional)
2. Basic Bible study and questions for discussion

3. Workshop activity—materials, activity, teacher "talking points" to be used
4. Wrap-up discussion/presentations
5. Closing prayer

The teacher "talking points" mentioned in item 3 above may include:

Teacher's personal reflections

Suggested comments

Questions for the class, such as:

How would you have . . . ?

What could you do to follow the teachings of this story in your life?

Suggested memory verse

Young grade modifications

Older grade modifications

Changes for age appropriateness should be included in each lesson plan, but we have found that our teachers, being mostly parents, naturally make these adjustments on their own, week to week. With younger children, we simplify the activities and schedule in extra help as needed for certain workshops. Often the lesson plan isn't 100 percent complete until the rotation coordinator and the actual workshop teacher have met.

Our teachers have much to contribute. Working with them, rather than just handing the lesson plan to them, allows for the exchange of ideas and helps the teacher better understand the focus of the rotation. Teachers are often inspired a week or two into the rotation. Thus, we go back to them near the end of the rotation to capture their improvements for posterity.

The remainder of this chapter is a sample of one five-week rotation, including schedule, overview, and lesson plans.

THE EXODUS—TELLING THE *WHOLE* STORY

ROTATION SCHEDULE

	Week 1	**Week 2**	**Week 3**	**Week 4**	**Week 5**
Grade 1	Audiovisual	Temple	Drama	Computer	Art
Grade 2	Drama	Audiovisual	Temple	Art	Computer
Grade 3	Computer	Art	Audiovisual	Drama	Temple
Grade 4	Temple	Computer	Art	Audiovisual	Drama
Grade 5/6	Art	Drama	Computer	Temple	Audiovisual

The possible configurations are as many as you can imagine. A four-week rotation with five classes would simply eliminate the fifth-week workshop. Thus, kids would miss one workshop per rotation. In a church with only three grade groups but five workshops, two of the workshops would be empty on any given week. You can view two other examples of workshop schedules in chapter 9.

Rotation Overview

Our six-year plan teaches the exodus story in four rotations. This rotation emphasizes sequencing the whole story of the exodus and the hardships endured. Map work is a great way to help students visualize and organize the progression of the story. Other exodus rotations include the call of Moses, crossing the Red Sea, and the Ten Commandments.

Audiovisuals Workshop

Story/Theme/Focus: Overall exodus story sequence

Learning Activity: Video clips from *The Ten Commandments,* with questions

Art Workshop

Story/Theme/Focus: Geography of the exodus

Learning Activity: Relief map with features of the exodus in non-drying clay

Computer Workshop

Story/Theme/Focus: Exodus sequencing through geography

Learning Activity: Interactive maps followed by computer quiz on story sequence

Drama Workshop

Story/Theme/Focus: Exodus story sequencing

Learning Activity: High-intensity "seven emotional exodus episodes"

Temple Workshop

Story/Theme/Focus: Exodus story sequencing

Learning Activity: Making jigsaw puzzle of exodus events

Lesson Plans

Here are the individual lesson plans for each of the five workshops. They are brief. During a meeting with the teacher and a member of the design team, the plans are fleshed out with the teacher's input.

AUDIOVISUAL WORKSHOP

Bible References: Numbers 20; 27:18–23; Deuteronomy 34; Joshua 3–8; Exodus 3:1–12, 5:1–2, 7:20–11:10, 12:31, 14:15–16, 20:1–17, 32:1–20

Objectives: Students will watch part of *The Ten Commandments*, from the call of Moses to the mountain top of Sinai and the golden calf, to gain a broad overview of the story.

Lesson Plan:

1. Assemble the students and have them locate the books of Exodus and Joshua in their Bibles. Point

out various sections in the story and tell them they will be seeing part of the story in the movie today.

2. Show the selected segments of the film. Edit or fast forward through the nonbiblical, "Hollywood" stuff. Follow up viewing with these questions:
   a. How did Moses feel when he saw the burning bush?
   b. Do you think it would be scary to hear the voice of God speaking to *you?*
   c. How did Moses react to God's call to go to Pharaoh? How would you have reacted?
   d. Do you think you would be willing to do whatever God tells you to do?
   e. How did Moses react to the people's unfaithfulness with the golden calf?
   f. How do you suppose God feels when you don't obey him?
3. Finish up the lesson by asking the children to list on the board as many parts of the exodus story as they can remember. Ask them to place the scenes they saw today in the correct order on their list. If you have time, you could make this a contest between two or three groups.

DRAMA WORKSHOP—EXODUS

Bible References: Numbers 20; 27:18–23; Deuteronomy 34; Joshua 3–8

Objective: Through dramatic interactive reenactment, students will gain a better understanding of the sequence of the story. Emotional aspects of the journey will be highlighted by the teacher asking the actors questions like, "What are you thinking about now, Moses?" The difficulties the Israelites experienced should also be highlighted.

Lesson Plan: Before the students arrive, make a list of the various scenes the students will reenact: the call, Moses and Pharaoh, Passover/plagues, the exodus, the Ten Commandments, Joshua, wandering, Moses' death.

1. Begin by asking the class to find the references in their Bibles to each of these scenes. Explain that the seven vignettes will take place in the four corners of the room: Mount Sinai, Pharaoh's court, the desert, at a home in Egypt. Give God a special area (hide a student under a sheet with a microphone for a nice booming effect!).

2. Assign parts for the drama: God, Moses, Pharaoh, Aaron, Joshua, Israelites. Let them get props and costumes together and set up the four corners of the room. This setup time is also a time for learning through discussion. Once they have their costumes and props, have the group first read through the four stories. Remind them that they will be moving quickly from scene to scene and be responsible for initiating dialogue, depending on their character's role (it may take a few minutes for them to get the idea).

3. After the initial read-through, the students go to the first corner, Bibles in hand, and reenact the scene with as much flair as possible. Ask some questions of the characters and then have them move to the next corner. Remind them that they are not putting on a show. Instead, they are directing it, discussing possible dialogue, and offering suggestions. Let them do a standing dry run, if necessary. During this dry run, you should be ready to prompt the actors with questions such as, "OK, then what did Pharaoh do?" and "What are you thinking now Moses?" "Crowd, what are you thinking at this moment?" This style of directing is called interactive drama.

4. After the students have moved through all four corners, challenge them to run through all the vignettes, giving only thirty seconds to each, but trying to get all the dialog in. Ask them to intensify the emotional nature of the scene.

5. Wrap up the activity by gathering everyone to discuss the one or two key questions and emotions that were identified during the drama. Discuss the nature of following God and how sometimes it is difficult.

BIBLE COMPUTER LAB

Bible References: Numbers 20; 27:18–23; Deuteronomy 34; Joshua 3–8

Objectives: Students will use maps and a worksheet to trace the exodus route and gain new information about locations along that route.

Lesson Plan:

1. Begin with face-to-face Bible study. Look for an exodus map in the back of the classroom Bible. Discuss the location of the exodus route in relationship to Israel, Egypt, and surrounding countries.
2. Pass out the Exodus Map Worksheet and explain how the software map operates. The worksheet lists many places along the exodus route. Students will explore the computer map to discover what happened at each of these locations and then record them on the worksheet. Students will find out how long the route was and how far Mount Sinai was from Egypt. Let older students complete the worksheet in groups of two at each computer. Cluster younger students and early readers in groups of three with a lab assistant, letting each student take a turn at using the computer or reading.
3. Come back together as a group and see what answers people came up with. Expound just a bit on what happened at those exodus locations.
4. Send them back to their computers to complete an exodus quiz. If you have time, let the class play the exodus computer game at the end of class.

TEMPLE WORKSHOP (BIBLE SKILLS AND GAMES)

Bible References: Numbers 20; 27:18–23; Deuteronomy 34; Joshua 3–8

Objectives: Students will create a puzzle that correctly sequences the exodus story. Students will be able to identify at least six events that occurred during Moses' life in correct order.

Lesson Plan:

1. Have each student name one thing she or he remembers about the exodus story. Write it all down on the board. Do not offer any guidance yet. Assign one of these references to each student, who is to look it up in the Bible and report the reference to the class in detail. If the students have missed any important parts of the exodus story, add those to their list (see list below).

Ex. 3:1–12	Call of Moses
Ex. 5:1–2	Pharaoh says no
Ex. 7:20–11:10	Ten plagues
Ex. 12:31	Pharaoh says go
Ex. 14:15–16	Parting of the sea
Ex. 20:1–17	The Ten Commandments
Ex. 32:1–20	Golden calf
Num. 27:18–23	Joshua
Deuteronomy 34	Moses sees the Promised Land

2. Give each student a blank assembled puzzle (available from catalogs) and round templates to draw nine circles on their puzzle (younger children may draw only six larger circles). In the middle of the puzzle, have them write "Moses and the Exodus." At the bottom they write "Exodus to Joshua." In each of the circles, have them illustrate, in order, the story scenes that they researched in step 1 above. Between each circle and

the next, have them write a "connecting phrase." Between circle 1 and circle 2, for example, the phrase might be "Moses goes to Pharaoh."

3. After the puzzles are complete, let the students take them apart and try to reassemble them. Send the puzzles home in baggies.

ART WORKSHOP

Bible References: Numbers 20; 27:18–23; Deuteronomy 34; Joshua 3–8

Objectives: Students will create modeling clay topographical maps of the exodus, using different colors and markers for important locations. They should focus on designing the topography to reflect the hardship of the exodus journey.

Lesson Plan:

1. As class begins, use a color map of the exodus route to conduct a brief discussion of what the children know about the exodus, where various parts of the story took place, and the general topography of that part of the world. As you are pointing to various areas, tell the stories of those locations.
2. Give each student a foam tray (the kind used for meat), and a supply of modeling clay (non-drying). Ask them to make a three-dimensional relief map of the exodus route. As they finish the initial map modeling, have them begin marking their maps with beads for important locations according to the legend (give each a "legend" handout). They tape the legend on the end of the foam tray so that it sticks up behind the map.

   As they work, offer comments to individuals and to the class as a whole about the exodus story related to the locations they are modeling and their choice of colors. Mountains, deserts, and seas all figure prominently in the story.

– 9 –

The Model in Small, Large, and Shared-Space Churches

The *Workshop Rotation Model* is proving extremely adaptable to churches of all sizes and to all sorts of facility limitations. The average church using the model has between five hundred and one thousand members. Rotation churches with fewer than five hundred members are coming on strong. The smallest church we know of doing the model has just over forty members. The largest rotation church has more than six thousand members; in fact, we know of two churches that size using it. In small and large churches the issue isn't so much what to teach as it is where to teach it and how much freedom you have to modify the rooms.

SMALL CHURCHES

Many small churches were not always that way—they have space to spare. Their rotations can be four or five weeks long with an equal number of workshops. The only difference is that they may only have two or three of the four or five workshops open on any given Sunday. Thus, teachers in this situation might have to teach their workshops only two or three times during the four- or five-week rotation. In some cases, the teachers sign up for two workshops. The first two weeks of the rotation they might staff the art workshop. The third and fourth weeks they might teach the audiovisual lesson.

The example that follows is a rotation schedule for two grade groups. There may indeed be five workshop rooms in the church. Or some of the rooms might pull double duty, such as the art room becoming the puppet room during week five and the audiovisual room becoming the Bible skills and games workshop. Notice also the option to put younger grades in a special puppet workshop while offering the older kids the Bible skills and games workshop.

	Week 1	**Week 2**	**Week 3**	**Week 4**	**Week 5**
Grades 1–3	Audiovisual	Computer	Newsroom	Art	Puppets
Grades 4–6	Computer	Audiovisual	Art	Newsroom	Bible skills

The following variation shows three grade groups with some special scheduling toward the end of the rotation.

	Week 1	**Week 2**	**Week 3**	**Week 4**	**Week 5**
Grades 1–2	Audiovisual	Newsroom	Computer	Art/music	Bible skills
Grades 3–4	Computer	Audiovisual	Newsroom	Bible skills	Art
Grades 5–6	Newsroom	Computer	Audiovisual	Art/music	Special Worship

Some small churches have very limited space. We know of two that conduct their workshops in the fellowship hall. Churches with limited space convert their one or two rooms into a different workshop each week. Large bins and plenty of cabinet space give them the storage for their workshop needs. (Art supplies, costumes, props, and puppets take up a *lot* of space.) An array of creative decor changes can transform an audiovisual workshop to drama quite easily. Quick changes often involve curtains, painted theater flats (painted for a different workshop on each side), tents, bolts of cloth hung across the ceiling, a roll of carpeting, and rearranged furniture.

Small churches often don't have a Christian education staff. While this may seem to make starting something new a daunting challenge, in fact, the *Workshop Rotation Model* is in some ways easier to implement in a small church than the traditional model. For one thing, the rotation model recruits from a wider circle of potential teachers. It also offers a respite from an expensive curriculum. Creativity and commitment are not lacking in small churches, and neither are the skills necessary to write good lessons. What's often lacking is a key person to whom others turn to for leadership and support. In larger churches this is the staff person.

Smaller churches will need to identify this "point person." One advantage small churches have in implementing the *Workshop Rotation Model* is the size of their classes. Creating a theater workshop or computer lab for four or five kids is much easier and less expensive than for a larger church with fifteen or more kids per group.

LARGE CHURCHES

Large churches often have very large numbers of kids, perhaps twenty-five or more students per class. Some very large churches may even have two classes or more for each grade group. Large churches may need six or more workshops just to keep the class sizes manageable. One limiting factor in your design and schedule is the right amount of time to spend on each story. Four to six weeks seems to be the consensus. Any more and the focus on the one Bible story starts to wear a little thin. In a large church with more than six class groupings, some of the classes will have to miss some of the workshops. For example, in a church that needs to create eight workshops to handle eight class groups, every group will miss three of the workshops in a five-week rotation period.

One way around this is to create two of almost everything: two art workshops, two audiovisual workshops, two computer labs. This allows a four- or five-week rotation period with more than four or five classes. Some workshops don't need to be doubled, however; they just need a larger room for two grade groups to share. The audiovisual Workshop is a good example. You can always handle an extra bunch of kids in that workshop, especially if the screen image is projected on the wall for everyone to see. One week in the rotation, two groups share the audiovisual workshop. The next week they go to separate workshops, while another two groups come into the audiovisual workshop. Of course, the beauty of the rotation model is that you determine the number of workshops, class sizes, and the length of the rotation period to fit *your* circumstances and facility. How should you plan? The correct answer is, plan what works for you, your kids, and your teachers, while keeping to the central tenets of the *Workshop Rotation Model.*

SHARED SPACE

Few other issues affect the Sunday school's psyche and facility like having to share space with a daycare or other community program. For many years, churches have just assumed that they had to accommodate these programs and their room needs. In fact, you could make the case that churches have given away too much. There are churches that cannot have religious pictures or symbols in their own classrooms.

Then there is the clash of equipment, furniture, and secular wall decorations. How do you turn a daycare room into a drama workshop on Sunday? What do you do with the sand table and room full of little chairs? Where will Alcoholics Anonymous meet if we convert "their" room into a computer lab? The solutions are not easy. They frequently involve a bit of soul-searching and tug-and-pull.

We were lucky in Barrington. We had the Christian education facility to ourselves. But ever since the *Workshop Rotation Model* began to spread, churches have been coming up with some very creative solutions to their shared-space problems. Here are just a few:

> Preschool lessons and activities typically rotate between stations within a room. Some churches have gotten together with their preschools and

created workshops for the preschool as well as the Sunday school.

Theater flats with murals on them are pulled out to block certain areas, walls, and equipment.

Tents can be quickly assembled each Sunday in the middle of a classroom. Once inside, the students don't notice that they're really in a preschool room.

Curtains of bright cloth are used to cordon off areas and block unsightly walls. Short of having these professionally made and installed, curtains can be sewn and strung along stiff wire using grommets or shower hooks.

Space is reclaimed as "Sunday school only." Some rotation churches have simply asked their preschools to consolidate (nature abhors a vacuum, and preschools abhor unused space) or move.

Last but not least, some churches find unused space. It may not have four walls, but it could be a very creative workshop space. Computer labs can pop up in the church library or at the end of a hallway. While not a terribly exciting space, the corner of the fellowship hall can become home to the audiovisual workshop, with a couple of dividers around it to reduce outside distractions. Many churches utilize a stage area as a workshop.

There is no perfect solution to implementing the *Workshop Rotation Model* in a shared space if the program sharing your facility refuses to change or cannot change, and if you aren't allowed to implement space-modifying solutions such as those mentioned above. And yet we've heard of many Sunday schools up against just such a problem. The issue really isn't space, it's mission. Space issues need to be tackled within an understanding of the congregation's primary mission: evangelism. Preschool programs and Scout troops do not evangelize. They are wonderful groups, but they do not carry the church into the next generation.

In cases where coexistence is difficult or impossible, the Sunday school must be the church's top priority. This is hard for some churches to accept, especially if there is rental income involved. The irony is that if the Sunday school isn't the church's priority, many church buildings may indeed become community centers in the next generation or two.

What Churches Are Saying about the *Workshop Rotation Model*

The boys went dashing down the hallway one Sunday morning. As they passed me, I asked, "Why are you in such a hurry?" Their reply: "We're going to Computer Lab!"

Never in my thirty-five years as a pastor have I seen children as excited about Sunday school as they are about our "God's Opening Doors" Rotation program.

—Dr. Tom Martin, Pastor, Memorial Presbyterian Church, Xenia, Ohio

Our adults have been most greatly affected by our change to the *Workshop Rotation Model.* Many of them, for the first time, are understanding that children, and all people, learn in different ways. They are supportive of and upbeat about the opportunities for children to experience the stories of the Bible in exciting ways. We have a much easier time getting leaders for Sunday school with workshops. Men and women who haven't taught before are willing to use their particular gifts as leaders of workshops. A cooking workshop leader, after teaching about the miracle at Cana, when Jesus turned water into wine (and workshop participants squeezed their own grape juice), said that her experience was "even more spiritual than when I was ordained an elder."

—Jackie Nowak, Director of Christian Education, Memorial Presbyterian Church, Xenia, Ohio

The *Workshop Rotation Model* responds to the needs of children, teachers, and the church better than any other model. It holds great promise for nurturing biblically literate children in this generation. True, we cover fewer stories in a church school year. However, the stories we do present are uncovered much more thoroughly and effectively.

—*Rev. Don Griggs, Westminster Presbyterian Church, Sacramento, California*

There is no question that more young people are joining our church because of what is happening in the children's wing.

—*David Pead, elder in charge of new members, Palma Ceia Presbyterian Church, Tampa, Florida*

It's great to see children and the whole family excited about Sunday school again. And most gratifying for me personally is that I don't have to spin my wheels recruiting teachers. They love it and just keep coming back for more.

—*Linda Beckham, Palma Ceia Presbyterian Church, Tampa, Florida*

About eight years ago I began to have second thoughts about our approach to Sunday school here at the Spirit of Hope. Our format, curriculum, and teaching methods left much to be desired. As a Christian Educator I faced the same recruiting and erratic attendance problems that many of my colleagues faced. The most critical concern for me was the overall lack of biblical literacy I was seeing in the children who had gone through the system. Sunday school, as we were conceptualizing it, was not engaging our children in a way that was stimulating them to learn at their best. I began to dream of a new approach that would incorporate cutting-edge media and technology. For several years visions of a media center with video, computers, and a drama production studio danced in my head with no realistic way to actualize it. Then in March of 1996, a colleague showed me an article about the *Workshop*

Rotation Model. It was an epiphany! Since we implemented the rotation model, the results have been astounding. Our Sunday school registration doubled the first year, and growth continues to exceed our expectations this year. Biblical literacy has dramatically increased as children retain the stories of faith and their implications for today. What a wonderful journey these past two years have been. It has taken a substantial investment in time, energy, and financial resources, but the blessings abound. Children and their families are really excited about Sunday school. New families are being attracted in record numbers. Most important, the faith story is coming alive for another generation. Our only "problem" has been parents having to literally drag their children from our Discovery Zones. I jokingly asked one little boy if I would have to lock him out of the Church Mouse (computer lab), and he shot back with, "Couldn't you just lock me in?!" What a wonderful problem to have.

—Ardys Sabin, former Christian Educator at Spirit of Hope United Methodist Church, Minneapolis, Minnesota

After being hired as a Director of Christian Education in my church, I remember saying, "I have no plans to do anything radical to the Sunday school." But after watching the program for a while, I knew something had to be done, or we would have not Sunday school in five years. In our first five months with the *Workshop Rotation Model,* we have seen not only an increase in attendance, but also in attention and retention as well.

—Karen Kriner, First Presbyterian, Macomb, Illinois

We needed something to add a spark to our Sunday morning program. Kids were here, but many because their parents made them come, not because they wanted to be here. It's hard to teach a group of kids who resent being here, and consequently, they learn little. The children's ministry committee presented our proposal to the session and, when they approved it, we began immediately to invite the congregation to be a part of the changeover process. I was amazed at their support! People who had never been a part of our department before offered to lead a rotation. Others offered their wonderful talents in art or carpentry to convert the rooms. Some gave gifts of money and others gifts of baskets, pottery, VCRs, and microwaves.

The biggest change I've seen in children is in their attitude. They love being here! When one family had tickets to see the Kansas City Chiefs play, a child cried because he wanted to go to Sunday school! I have never heard of that in my entire career. Other families have told us that the children's friends ask if they can spend the night on Saturday night so that they can go to Sunday school with them on Sunday morning!

Not only do they enjoy being here, but when we quiz them on the last Sunday of a rotation, I am amazed at what they have learned. The thing that appeals to me most about this model is the engagement of the children. We have had many visitors from other churches come on Sunday morning to observe our program. When we walk into a room, the children are so engaged in their activity that they hardly notice we're there.

As an educator, I find it much easier to get folks to commit to teaching for five or six weeks rather than for nine months. And they're able to sign up for a rotation where they feel comfortable.

—Judy Cooper, Director of Children's Ministry, Village Presbyterian Church, Prairie Village, Kansas

Beginning the workshop approach has done more than create excitement in our church. It has captured the spotlight for Christian education and made it clear that Sunday school can actually be a keystone ministry that draws new and unchurched families into our fellowship. In addition to a 23 percent sustained increase in attendance, there is objective evidence that Zion students are retaining the biblical life lessons we are teaching through this approach. For us, that's what defines a successful ministry. Our parents also let us know we're on the right track by telling stories of the impact our workshops have had on their sons and daughters.

One parent commented to me that her son was getting ready for Sunday school two hours before it was time to go because he was so excited to be a part of the program. We're a congregation that is blessed to have caught this vision of ministry. It honors the Lord by opening hearts to hear the gospel in new and magnetic ways!

—Cliff Heagy, Director of Youth and Outreach, Zion United Church of Christ, Sheboygan, Wisconsin

Sunday school, as most of us have known it, does not seem to be doing the job we want it to do in many churches today. The *Workshop Rotation Model* is certainly not the only answer for what ails the Sunday school. But it does address a number of concerns and does it well. It creates opportunities for more adults to be involved in educational ministry in ways that tap into their particular skills and interests. Consequently, children and youth may develop relationships with a wider range of adults. And the model builds on what we know about how people learn by providing many ways for students to be actively engaged in the learning process. I tell my students that the *Workshop Rotation Model* is labor intensive. But, then, most worthwhile things in this world are.

—Dr. Diane J. Hymans, Associate Professor of Christian Education, Trinity Lutheran Seminary, Columbus, Ohio

— 11 —

Getting Started

After our "flip chart inspiration" and approval from church leadership, we transformed our Sunday school over the summer. Summer is a popular time to make the switch. Schedules and attendance are usually different, and in some churches there is no Sunday school at all. We created two workshops a month, so that by September we had six ready to go. It took us about two or three rotation periods to work the kinks out and help our teachers get comfortable. Other churches report a similar experience.

Some rotation churches have designed their vacation Bible school to use workshops. At the end of the week, they left the workshops up for the Sunday school to start using. This gave them extra time to devote to design team curriculum planning. Quite a few churches were inspired mid-year to convert to rotation, while others have chosen the season of Advent as a time to get started. One church in Jamestown, New York, thought they would "give it a try" during Lent, when the congregation expected special programming. Their teachers, parents, and kids were so happy with the Lent rotation that they immediately scheduled another and never looked back.

While our workshops looked great from day one, we still kept adding to them bit by bit. If nobody has laid claim to the phrase "decorating on the cheap," we'd like to. Of course, we spent money on things like paint and art stools, but we were not spending thousands of dollars on curriculum either. And when we did need to spend money, people were supportive, knowing that something special was happening downstairs.

Change usually begins with just a few people and a shared vision. Helping others capture that enthusiasm and vision can be a challenge in some churches. Rather than focusing on the nuts and bolts of the *Workshop Rotation Model,* we recommend thoughtfully engaging church leaders, teachers, and parents in a soul-searching confessional exercise, such as the one we engaged in with our leaders. Establish a consensus about the problems you are facing and the fact that change is needed. Once you've done that, the next step is to brainstorm or to introduce a model that addresses people's needs and concerns. Often, the only thing needed to produce enthusiasm and support in a congregation is a really good idea that appeals to many different needs, doesn't cost a lot of money, and promises results. For our congregation and many others, that really good idea is the *Workshop Rotation Model.*

God Bless!

RESOURCES

www.rotation.org

Probably the best place to start looking for more rotation resources is the official *Workshop Rotation Model* website: www.rotation.org. There you will find information about a rotation newsletter, more than two dozen free lesson sets, articles, and seminar information. The site contains a message board for rotation educators to share ideas and expertise. You'll also find links to published rotation resources and recommended rotation curriculum publishers. Rotation.org is a not-for-profit ecumenical site managed and financed by a number of rotation churches.

Resource Centers

Your local Christian resource center or bookstore has an extensive collection of teaching materials that can be adapted for *Workshop Rotation Model* use.

Workshop-Specific Resources

Here is a sampling of workshop-specific Christian education resources we have found helpful in our Sunday school.

Art

Arts and Activities. This magazine not only reviews new art materials, it contains lesson plans written by art teachers. Subscription Manager, 591 Camino de la Reina, Suite 200, San Diego, CA 92108, (619) 297-8032.
Mudworks, by Mary Ann F. Kohl. The author shares many excellent art projects and includes clear instructions. Bright Ring Publishing Inc., PO Box 31338, Bellingham, WA 98228-3338, (800) 480-4278.
The Art of Teaching and *The Art Project Calendar,* by Sandra Woodworth. Great art projects and lesson plans. Show & Tell Productions, PO Box 322, Perrysburg, OH 43551.
Art Supply Catalogs: Sax Arts & Craft, (800) 558-6696.

Audiovisual

Critic's Choice Video, (800) 367-7765
Gateway Films, (800) 523-0226
Nest Entertainment, (972) 402-7100

Computer Lab

Sunday School Software Ministries: software catalog, how-to book, teaching materials, (800) 678-1948, www.sundaysoftware.com.
Scroll magazine, software reviews and articles, Deerhaven Press, PO Box 603, Versailles, KY 40383-0603, (800) 961-0015.

Drama

Anderson's Prom and Party Catalog: backdrops, palm trees, cardboard pillars, (800) 896-2353
Contemporary Drama Service: plays and books, (800) 937-5287
Drama Workshop Manual: in the free lessons section at www.rotation.org.

Puppets

Folkmanis Puppets: good quality animal hand puppets, (510) 658-7677.
One Way Street: all sorts of puppets and puppet supplies, including Bible-Time Puppets, (800) 569-4537.

Miscellaneous Workshop Resources

Hannaford, Carla. *Smart Moves: Why Learning Is Not All in Your Head*. Arlington, Va.: Great Ocean Publishers, 1995.
Lefever, Marlene. *Learning Styles*. Elgin, Ill.: David C. Cook Publishing, 1996. A terrific book on understanding learning styles in a Sunday school setting.
Smith, Jeff. *The Frugal Gourmet Keeps the Feast*. New York: William Morrow & Co., 1995.
Whitcomb, Holly W. *Feasting with God: Adventures in Table Spirituality*. Cleveland: United Church Press, 1996.